Young

2004 POETRY C

ONCE UPON A RHYME

IMAGINATION FOR
A NEW GENERATION

West Country Vol III
Edited by Donna Samworth

 Young**Writers**

First published in Great Britain in 2004 by:
Young Writers
Remus House
Coltsfoot Drive
Peterborough
PE2 9JX
Telephone: 01733 890066
Website: www.youngwriters.co.uk

SB ISBN 1 84460 547 7

Foreword

Young Writers was established in 1991 and has been passionately devoted to the promotion of reading and writing in children and young adults ever since. The quest continues today. Young Writers remains as committed to engendering the fostering of burgeoning poetic and literary talent as ever.

This year's Young Writers competition has proven as vibrant and dynamic as ever and we are delighted to present a showcase of the best poetry from across the UK. Each poem has been carefully selected from a wealth of *Once Upon A Rhyme* entries before ultimately being published in this, our twelfth primary school poetry series.

Once again, we have been supremely impressed by the overall high quality of the entries we have received. The imagination, energy and creativity which has gone into each young writer's entry made choosing the best poems a challenging and often difficult but ultimately hugely rewarding task - the general high standard of the work submitted amply vindicating this opportunity to bring their poetry to a larger appreciative audience.

We sincerely hope you are pleased with our final selection and that you will enjoy *Once Upon A Rhyme West Country Vol III* for many years to come.

Contents

Leigh Spurle (11)   19
Caroline Skeggs (11)   20
Jacob Kahan (10)   21
Terri Samways (11)   22
Gemma Taylor (11)   23
Joshua Brett (11)   24
Kristian White (11)   25
Aaron Neal (11)   26
Siân Andrews (11)   27
Matthew Bollen (11)   28
Lauren Green (11)   29
Gemma Lawrence (10)   30
George Gulliford (10)   31
Daniel Robinson (10)   32
Paula Wright (10)   33
Bobby Webb (11)   34
Callum Shortland (10)   35
Christopher Priddle (11)   36

Heytesbury CE Primary School, Warminster

Sasha Bowen (10)   36
Eris Harland (10)   37
Sarah Hand (9)   37
Rebecca Newman (10)   38
Kelly Ann Mitchell (10)   38
Poppy Nicol (10)   39
Emma Reade (9)   40
Stephen Shuster (10)   41
Jasmine Kate Lindsay (10)   42
Shana Lewis (9)   43
Matthew Bone (8)   44
Harry Howlett (9)   44
Jamie McDougall (11)   45
Lauren Pinnell (9)   45
Rebecca Schofield (9)   46
Joel Hart (7)   46
Anabel Giessler (8)   47
Lottie Hedley-Harper (8)   47
Jessica Agate (9)   48
Kiya Burgess (8)   48
Jake Coward (7)   48

Heather Newman (10)   49

Holway Park Primary School, Taunton
David White (9)   49
William Massingham (9)   50
Matthew Cross (8)   50
Max Salter (8)   51
Rebecca Williams (8)   51
Rory Grant (8)   51
Jordan Jones (8)   52
Pagan Ferguson (8)   52
Rhiannon Swateridge (8)   52
Grant Adams (11)   53
Shannon Carp (9)   53
Hannah Cook (9)   54
Joseph Coombes   54
Amy Ward (7)   55
Lauren Jones (8)   55
Joshua Bartlett (8)   56
Leah Musgrove (8)   56
Phoebe Scarborough (8)   57
Chloe Snell (8)   57
Marcus Alba (11)   58
Dominic Walding (8)   58
Claire Ryan (9)   59
Casey Harris (9)   59
Sally Alexander (11)   60
Anthony Millar (10)   61
Darren Pring (8)   61
Serena Spiller (11)   62
Ashley Carter (7)   63
Harley Collard (9)   63
Georgia Allen (7)   64

Horsington CE Primary School, Templecombe
Briony Smith (7)   64
Sam Fox (8)   65
Jonti Allinson-Epps (8)   65
Lewis Godfrey-Cuff (8)   65
Luke Wagland (8)   66
Olivia Clayton (8)   66

James Antell (9)	67
Bethany Coffin (7)	67
Lucy Wingate (8)	68
Toby Wagstaff (7)	68
Emma Mylan (8)	69
Joe Miller (8)	69
Harry Coates (7)	70
Alex Harvey (8)	70

Keevil CE Primary School, Trowbridge

Rory Harrison (8)	71
David Vick (8)	71
Ben Streeter (7)	72
Daniel Streeter (10)	72
Claire Harbour (8)	73
Jessica Nurdin (10)	73
Donna Turner (8)	74
George Caine (8)	74
Jacob Case (7)	75
Clarissa Reid (8)	75
Charlotte Richardson (8)	76
Bertie Smith (10)	76
Joshua Dobson (8)	77
William Locke (8)	77
Georgina Richardson (11)	78
Luke Tyler (7)	78
Sam Smith (9)	79
Josh Baker (9)	80
Thomas Meade (9)	81
Natasha Parsons (10)	81
Isabel Breach (9)	81
Rebecca Tyler (10)	82
Gemma Nurdin (9)	83

Norton Fitzwarren CE VC Community School, Taunton

Amy Bond (10)	83
Olivia Pring (10)	84
Robert Stewart (10)	84
Josh Mattravers (10)	85
Kira Lamb (11)	85
Lloyd Cotton (8)	86

Ryan Hallett (10)   86

Parkfield Primary School, Taunton
Alexander Izzard (9)   86
Holly Ashford (10)   87
Ruby Kite (10)   88
Joshua Miller (10)   89
Emily Baker (10)   89
Jasmine Ballardie (10)   90
Zoe Oliver (8)   90
Andrew Beaumont (10)   91
Aaron Macdonald (10)   91
Joseph Brown (10)   92
Hannah Lucas (9)   92
Sophie Cox (10)   93
Abigail Stone (9)   93
Emily Dunningham (10)   94
Thomas Stevens (9)   94
Rebecca Elies (9)   95
Hannah Kemp (9)   95
Ashley Lamb (10)   95
Tess Gillham (10)   96
Sophie Morgan (10)   96
Robert Hayes (10)   97
Amy Howes (8)   97
Ellie Kidsley (9)   98
Jamie-Lee Cosgree (8)   98
Saffron Robertson (9)   99
Jonathan Limm (10)   99
Kimberley McEvansoneya (10)   100
James Browning (8)   100
Lydia Murphy (10)   101
Harriet Walsh (8)   101
Bethan Rayner (10)   102
Kelly York (10)   102
Eleanor Roderick (9)   103
Russell Gilbert (10)   103
Michael Ying (10)   104
Amelia Salmon (10)   104
Jessica Fryer-Sims (10)   105
Adam Salter (10)   105

Georgina Trick (10)	106
Elliot Cook (11)	106
Charlotte Upton (9)	107
Daniel Cowans (10)	107
Duncan John Verwey (10)	108
David Brawn (10)	108
Ana-Maria Williams (10)	109
Lucy White (9)	109
Ashleigh Russell (8)	110
Emily Cooke (10)	110
Darren Cooper (10)	111
Laura Alison (10)	112
Jordan Ireland (9)	112
Sophie Groves (11)	113
Elliott Norman (9)	113
Lydia Osborne (10)	114
Richard Frazer (10)	114
Bethany Power (9)	115
Rory Tomlinson (11)	115
Jack Turner (11)	116
Isabelle Mott (11)	116
Sophie Hatchett (10)	117
Nathan Wilson (8)	117
Elspeth Rudd (11)	118
Tom Bates (11)	118
Lauren England (9)	119
James Barton (11)	119
Tobias Summerill (8)	120
Grant Whitear (11)	120
Robyn Kidsley (11)	121
Lindsay Knutt (8)	121
Edith Humphries (8)	122
Hannah Frounks (8)	122
Georgia Davey (8)	122
Sophie Knutt (9)	123

Peasedown St John Primary School, Bath

Sarah Lanning (8)	123
Alice Graham (8)	124

Portishead Primary School, Portishead

Priddy Primary School, Wells

St Julian's Primary School, Bath

Wells Cathedral Junior School, Wells

Cervinia Wakelin-Gilden (11)   195
Alexander Goodliff (10)   196
Alice Laing (10)   197
Timothy Coppen (10)   198
James Brand (11)   199
Ella Kelly (11)   200
Samantha Peirce (10)   201
Georgia Geipel (10)   202
Jessica Orrett (10)   203
Alexander Hopperton (10)   203
Sorcha Kennedy (10)   204

West Chinnock CE Primary School, Crewkerne
Jade Redfern (9)   204
Kerry Roberts (10)   205
Becky Doherty (11)   205
Joe Leighton (11)   205
Jack Hawker (11)   205
Sarah-Jane Nicholson (11)   206

West Coker CE VC Primary School, Yeovil
Denis Cozens (7)   206
Christopher Townsend (10)   206
Sarah Fudge (9)   207
Dale Antcliffe (9)   207
Jade Whittle (10)   207
Sophie Hackett (9)   208
Harriet Eason (11)   208
Tom Sollars (10)   208
Sarah Brady (9)   209
Louise Goodland (10)   209
Alexandra Barbaro (11)   209
Jack Cozens (10)   210
Jared Wiseman (11)   210
Sam Harris (9)   210
Chloe Partridge (8)   211
Jim Crisp (11)   211
Bran Pick (7)   212
Khan Green (7)   212
Elliot Boon (9)   213
Amy Reddaway (9)   213

Robert Small (7)   214
Niki Thiella (8)   214
Daisy Copland (9)   214
Molly Morris (7)   215

Weston Park Primary School, Lawrence Weston
Sarah Campbell (9)   215
Ewan Estcourt (9)   216
Ceri-Mai Shepherd (9)   216
Kara Houson (8)   217
Jacob Hicks (8)   217
Alex McGill (9)   218
Lauren Ogden (8)   218
Kirsty Hannan (9)   218
Hannah Weekes (9)   219
Callum James (9)   219

Wiveliscombe Primary School, Taunton
Esther Watson (9)   220
Charlie Mitchell (8)   221
Sophie Prescott (9)   222
Rachael Bashford (10)   222
Jessica Robinson (10)   223
Laura Vercoe (11)   223
Zoe Wilkes (10)   224
Andrew Fudge (9)   224
Rosie Johnson (9)   225
Ben Salter (8)   225
Vicky Bendall (10)   226
Fiona Hamilton (10)   226
Jack Cowling (10)   227
Steven Grabham (10)   227
Jack Humphries (10)   228
Hannah Stone (11)   228
Andrew Heard (10)   229
Rhianna White (10)   229

The Poems

Dreams

I can be about winter, I can be about peace,
I can be about turtles or about Greece,
I can be quite slow or really fast,
I can be about the future or the past,
I can be about water or swimming pools,
I can be about the moon or ghosts and ghouls,
I can be about pets or about a boat,
I can be about an adventure or about a golden coat,
I can be about the stars or about a mountain,
I can be about a secret garden or about a fountain,
I can be something special or about an earthquake,
I can be a castle surrounded by a lake,
When you turn in I always come,
I can be about anything, even your thumb.

Aimee Lines (10)
Box Highlands Primary School, Corsham

The Seasons

Winter, summer, autumn, spring
Those are the seasons that hide within
Year by year those seasons go by
Always gone in a blink of an eye
Spring with leaves, summer with sun
Autumn to chill, winter to come
Four of these in a year
Each one drawing near
What will happen when the seasons die?
Will they come to rest or hide?
Seasons are netted in a line
Good job we don't have nine.

Allan Lainchbury (10)
Box Highlands Primary School, Corsham

Fox

I prowl at night
I sleep when it's light
I love to play
But not when it's day
I hunt for deers
I live for years
I have sharp teeth
That are made to . . . *bite!*

Geraldine Garlick (9)
Box Highlands Primary School, Corsham

Cheetah

There is a cheetah
Who liked to pounce
She sleeps all night
And hunts all day
She never gives up
And never gives in
Until she catches her prey.

Elle McGuckien (10)
Box Highlands Primary School, Corsham

Food In The Sea

One day, I went to the beach,
I looked in the sea and found a peach.
This wasn't a normal peach you must see,
It was a peach full of dreams.
Then I found a chocolate bar
And found that it was full of tar.
Then I looked down right in the sea
And found bananas just like me.

Ellie Crosby (9)
Box Highlands Primary School, Corsham

Young Then Old

I'm a little baby, fat and chubby,
You wouldn't believe I came from my mummy.

Now I'm a schoolgirl learning in school,
When I came home, I found a dog in our pool.

Teenager I am, with a mobile phone,
Would you like to hear my phone ringtone?

Adult I am, near old age,
I just keep turning over the page.

I'm an old granny, sitting in my knitting chair,
My howling dog sounds like a bear.

Maizie Dick (9)
Box Highlands Primary School, Corsham

Winter

Remember the long, warm days of summer,
When butterflies danced a silent dance
Amongst the merry flowers.
Candy-pink mornings and rainbow evenings
When gentle love spread through the air.
But now the purple days are cold and short,
The icy moon peeps from behind the stormy clouds,
Will summer never return?

Isobel Ford (10)
Box Highlands Primary School, Corsham

Riddles

Five big poles connected together
They run on wind or whatever the weather
They make electricity and are very tall
They are in this country and in Cornwall.

Philip Edwards (10)
Box Highlands Primary School, Corsham

The Teacher

I once had a really horrible teacher
That tried to make my friend even weaker
She slapped my face
And untied my lace
I tripped over her foot
She smacked me with a book
Then I did a prank
On her boyfriend, Hank
She left the school
And headed to Nepal
And never came back again.

Thomas Barstow (10)
Box Highlands Primary School, Corsham

Kennings Feet Stomper

Feet stomper
Ground smasher
Horn blower
Water sucker
Mouse hater
Water blaster
Sound hearer
Smell sniffer
What am I?

Elephant.

Steven Watson (10)
Box Highlands Primary School, Corsham

The Lighthouse

One day there was a light
That appeared out of nowhere
Everyone said the lighthouse was haunted
But I didn't believe a word.

Whenever I looked
There was a figure at the top
Staring out to the moonlit pier
Pointing out to sea.

But when I turned around and looked back
He had gone.

Daniel Day (10)
Box Highlands Primary School, Corsham

Storm

I sometimes come but not all of the time
I'm in the air and all around
All dark and gloomy
What am I?

Moon
All big, sitting in the night
All alone, except tiny twinkles that glow
What am I?

Bird
I soar through the sky, I come in all types
I mostly come in black
What am I?

Daisy Fortt (9)
Box Highlands Primary School, Corsham

Fly Little Fly

I hover gracefully in the air,
Virtually invisible you'll think I wasn't there,
I zoom about living out my life,
My wings are razor blades, sharp as a knife.
I whizz about eating second-hand,
I live anywhere, even on the sand.
Annoying sometimes,
I only want to eat,
A group of me you wouldn't really want to meet.

Harley Oliff (10)
Box Highlands Primary School, Corsham

Summer

Imagine if I was summer
I would make everyone feel like a prince.

If I was a flower
I could make the day cheerful.

Perhaps if I was a butterfly
I could float through the summery gardens.

What if I flew from Africa
And spread my wings in the warm, balmy air?

Thomas Keeley (9)
Box Highlands Primary School, Corsham

Limerick

There was a man from Leeds
Who ate a packet of seeds
He fell into a drain
And got ran over by a train
And became a lump of weeds.

Peter Ammel (9)
Box Highlands Primary School, Corsham

The Cinema

I went to the cinema yesterday
I went to see Harry Potter
I sat in the seat, my hands on my feet
And I noticed that it was now hotter.

Now I had to go through the adverts
They really were boring as well
They had bottles of shampoo, an old man's tattoo
And a car that no one could sell.

Then I had a swig of fizzy
It gurgled into my mouth
The bubbles went *pop*, the fizzy did drop
Then out came the wind from down south.

Then comes the chorus of shushes
As darkness falls over the room
I just had to shiver, my lips were a-quiver
And I saw my dad's face in the gloom.

And then after a very long while
The movie had ended, oh no!
The fizzy was not in my system
I just had to go!

Now after a couple of minutes
We clambered into the car
The engine started roaring but this trip was boring
But that cinema screen's a real star!

Jason E Gray (11)
Grass Royal Junior School, Yeovil

The Magic Box

(Based on 'Magic Box' by Kit Wright)

I will put in my box . . .

A shiny, silver star out of space
A speck of the finest sand from the beach
The biggest crystal from the world's largest mountain
A memory of my grandad.

I will put in my box . . .

A sample of all the world's seas
My sister's first word
The first time I made a cup of tea.

I will put in my box . . .

My brother's first lick of an ice cream
My mum's first smile.

My box is made out of rubies and crystals for the outside
And clear ice for the hinges
There are memories in every corner of my magic box.

Shanna Molloy (10)
Grass Royal Junior School, Yeovil

In My Mind There Is . . .

In my mind there is anything that I want,
Like baby-blue skies with candyfloss clouds cluttered around.
There's the cool, refreshing splash of white sea foam
And the first lick of an ice cream cone.

But in my mind there are mad things too
Like seeing eternity in an hour
As you watch the reversed life cycle of a dying flower.
You can put the world in a grain of sand
And hold life and death in the palm of your hand.

But in my mind there is no war
And that is because it is bad
And makes me feel very sad.

Jacob A Ware (11)
Grass Royal Junior School, Yeovil

My Magic Box

(Based on 'Magic Box' by Kit Wright)

I will put in my box . . .

The soft snow on a winter's day
The brilliant breeze that sweeps around
The funny fantasy of Mr Bean.

I will put in my box . . .

The hover of a jet that flies through the air
The fluffy tail of my cat, Misty
A key to the gaming world.

I will put in my box . . .

A super cookie that never runs out
The fastest car in the world
And a big mansion.

My box is a glittering gold
That can never break.

Ben Loveridge (11)
Grass Royal Junior School, Yeovil

Down The Bottom Of The Garden

Down the bottom of the garden I dug up . . .
A family of pandas from the Antarctica
A sock I lost when I was three
And two sweets that once belonged to me.

Down the bottom of the garden I dug up . . .
The crown jewels left by the Queen
My missing homework from Year 5
And a big brother that once belonged to me.

Down the bottom of the garden I dug up . . .
Peter Pan from the Netherlands
A world I had never seen
And my mum, looking for me!

Jo Askew (11)
Grass Royal Junior School, Yeovil

My Secret Place

In my secret place is . . .

A glint of golden jewellery,
Hidden well away.
A silk bag full of natural shells,
Floating near the bay.

In my secret place is . . .

A glistening guitar,
Used by famous bands.
A china doll with shimmering clothes,
Kept with gentle hands.

In my secret place is . . .

Tinted windows spotlessly clean,
Giving a view for all to see.
All my friends are there,
Everyone . . . including *me!*

Leah Moger (11)
Grass Royal Junior School, Yeovil

My Point Of View

They leave me on my own, never ask me to play.
I'm getting bored, it's the same every day.
I stand there making patterns in the mud
Leaving prints behind.

They walk past me, giggling as they go.
I wonder what their joke is?
Teachers look at them smiling
Then they turn to me and their smile turns to a frown.

My point of view is, they don't like me.
So I don't like them!

Gemma Cuss (11)
Grass Royal Junior School, Yeovil

My Secret Room

In my secret room I have . . .

Three superheroes that help save the world and make it a better place.
They drive super cars that come from outer space.
A plant that grows money
And a parrot that talks rubbish.

In my room I have . . .

The Simpsons running wild,
Bart skateboarding, Lisa deafening everyone with her saxophone.
Marge telling Bart off for fighting with Lisa
And Homer saying, 'Mmm beer.'

In my room I have . . .

The England football team who have just won the World Cup.
Two World War II planes that defeated the Nazis
And got their victory.

I am the only one with the key to my room.
It's like Heaven and it's all mine.

Tom McAdam (11)
Grass Royal Junior School, Yeovil

Just Me!

Which career should I choose?
I could play football but then I'd lose.
I could be a lawyer but I fancy not.
Maybe a news reporter for 'Hot'.
But then again, I'm just me!

Holly Roberts (10)
Grass Royal Junior School, Yeovil

What If?

What if there was no grass?
What if there were no trees?
Oh, how hot it would be
If there wasn't any breeze.

What if there were no people?
What if there were no pets?
Imagine if we couldn't be cared for by doctors
And the animals couldn't get care from vets.

What if there were no countries,
Or no towns, woods or hills?
How would we have flour
If it couldn't be ground in the mills?

What if there were no seasons?
No summer, winter or spring,
Imagine the poor insects and birds,
If they didn't have any wings.

Stephen d'Albiac (11)
Grass Royal Junior School, Yeovil

Pocket Money

Kids get their pocket money from their mum or dad.
Some don't get it which makes them very sad.
Lots of kids spend it on lots of sweets.
Maybe some would buy a bird that goes *tweet.*
I would spend it on my favourite thing.
A Warhammer model which fires balls that go *ping.*
Teenagers might spend it on guitars or drums.
Or some might spend it on tobacco that rots your lungs.
Women waste their money on different shoes.
And sometimes they find it hard to choose.
Men might spend it on a football ticket.
But nevertheless, some still like cricket.

Morgan Grubb (11)
Grass Royal Junior School, Yeovil

The Magic Box

(Based on 'Magic Box' by Kit Wright)

I will put in the box . . .

A gold, glossy key that opens the world
The first day of school where I looked hot
But I was just embarrassed
My first scrumptious cooked dinner.

I will put in the box . . .

The day when I went to the shiny, bright beach of Spain
The day that Charles Darwin made the theory of evolution
The day that Albert Einstein made the theory of relativity.

I will put in the box . . .

The big red flame of hair on fire
The day my mum chucked a pudding
I shall always keep it in my pocket.

My magic box is made of gold and silver glass
With patterns and secrets around it.

James Walter (11)
Grass Royal Junior School, Yeovil

In My Special Box

(Based on 'Magic Box' by Kit Wright)

In my special box . . .
Is a trace of golden treasure
Shining silver and gold brightly in the sun
I take some for my own pleasure
Fun for everyone to play with
But you must put it back!

In my special box . . .
Are pink elephants dancing to a beat
So bright that they blind you
Stamping around with their enormous big feet
My box looking absolutely new
But you must put it back!

Kathryn Bellamy (11)
Grass Royal Junior School, Yeovil

My Secret Place

In my secret place . . .
There is an animal that no one knows.
A beach with sand as soft as velvet
And water that shimmers all year through.

In my secret, hidden place . . .
There is a key made especially for me.
A mountain of jewels that lay,
Glistening on the floor.

In my secret, hidden, special place . . .
There is a forest as peaceful as the twitter of birds
With a bed of flowers as bright as a rainbow.
Clouds as white as snow, scattered in the sky.

To get to my secret place . . .
You need the key
The key especially for me.

Heather Lambert (10)
Grass Royal Junior School, Yeovil

Shot Of A Lifetime

I am sat here waiting for my turn.
The sun is scorching, I hope I don't burn.
Now it is time for me to bat,
Have I remembered everything?
My pads, my gloves and my hat?
I walk across the pitch, the crowd claps as I pass,
I am stood at the wicket at last.
The ball comes flying in without a sound,
I hit the ball out of bounds.
'What a great shot!' shouted the crowd,
Winning the game made the whole team proud.

Matt Jackson (10)
Grass Royal Junior School, Yeovil

The Magic Box

(Based on 'Magic Box' by Kit Wright)

I will put in my box . . .

A wish for world peace
And for everyone to be happy.

I will put in my box . . .

The best yellow beach in the world
A sunset to make everyone happy.

I will put in my box . . .

The day I get a new friend.

I will put in my box . . .

The day Yeovil wins the World Cup.

My box is a magic box
Which is made of the shining light from the sun.

Toby Osborne (10)
Grass Royal Junior School, Yeovil

Writing Poems

I am trying to write a poem,
It's not that easy you see.
It is about a crime, it shall not rhyme,
Though this fly is bothering me.

It is buzzing around my head,
I need to write the date.
I just wish this fly was dead,
The robber is smashing a plate.

Great, I am stuck now,
I don't know what to write.
Should the policemen take a bow?
Out of the window there is a red kite.

Oh, now I know what to write!

Cori Attwell (11)
Grass Royal Junior School, Yeovil

My Hidden Mind

My hidden mind is full of dreams and scary thoughts
I've had things I hope to happen
And dreams I hope to have.

To sitting by the sea
With the fishes round my feet
To standing on the moon
With the rock upon my feet.

What I have inside
Is all my thoughts and tears
All my friends and secrets
And all my hidden fears.

Now I have to leave
Because I'm growing up
I hope to find another mind
To make my world complete.

Charlotte Darch (11)
Grass Royal Junior School, Yeovil

My Body Calls Me . . .

My heart calls me Thumper.
My bones call me Clicker.
My brain calls me Smart.
My eye calls me See.
My legs call me Lanky.
My nose calls me Smelly.
My stomach calls me Fatty.
My arms call me Flappy.
My fingers call me Bendy
And I call me Ashley!

Ashley Light (10)
Grass Royal Junior School, Yeovil

My Secret World

In my secret world . . .
The trees are made of lollipops,
The seas and rivers are made of chocolate milk
And the grass is made from icing.

In my secret world . . .
The rain is lemonade
And the sun is made from white chocolate.
There are sugar paper flowers
Which are planted in sherbet soil
And the sky is made from bubblegum.

In my secret world . . .
Everyone is friends,
No one ever falls out
Or is mean to one another.

In my secret world . . .
All my dreams and secrets
Are locked away in a drawer
And only I have a key.

But here I lie in my bed,
Too bad my world is in my head.

Jade Jackson (11)
Grass Royal Junior School, Yeovil

My Secret Wood

In my secret wood is . . .

A witch on a broom cackling.
Owls in the trees hooting.
Fireworks shoot up in the air crackling.
Silky spiderwebs scattered everywhere.

In my secret wood . . .

Over in the corner is a magic tree house.
It can turn you into animals.
Like an elephant or perhaps a mouse.
The tree house's ladder is made of candy cane.

In my secret wood . . .

Trees are made of chocolate
Leaves are sugar paper
The moon is made of cheese
And the stars are made of sherbet.

But here I sit in the classroom
I really wish I could be
In my secret wood.

Rebecca Maunder (11)
Grass Royal Junior School, Yeovil

In My Secret Place

In my secret place is a . . .
Piece of paper waiting
For my thoughts to
Jump on it.
In my secret place is a . . .
Dream floating around
Past the homework
Waiting to be done
Through the times table
Stuck away in my mind.
In my secret place is a . . .
Poem waiting to
Be written on paper.
In my secret place is a . . .
Crumb of intelligence
In a little pot.
But in my secret place there are . . .
Two entrances and when
Something goes in one
It usually goes out
Of the other.
My secret place is my mind . . .
But it is locked
And the key to it is
Me!

Leigh Spurle (11)
Grass Royal Junior School, Yeovil

The Magic Box

(Based on 'Magic Box' by Kit Wright)

I will put in the box . . .

A dolphin out in the deep blue ocean
With the sound of whales singing.

A unicorn's horn with secret powers
And
Buttercups gleaming yellow
Buttercups I always used to eat when I was a baby.

I will put in the box . . .

My first secret
That I told to my best friend in the playground
My first friend, Terri Samways
We met at playschool
And
A golden key to open my future.

I will put in the box . . .

The washing on my table
I thought was a monster.

The box that is mine
Is made of gold, ice and a see-through handle
And
The box will be kept under the pillow
Of my comfy bed.

Caroline Skeggs (11)
Grass Royal Junior School, Yeovil

The Magic Box

(Based on 'Magic Box' by Kit Wright)

I will put in the box . . .

A black horse galloping across the mystical moon.
When my first tear was shed.
A stripy tiger cub to play with.
A hug from my black, furry dog.

I will put in the box . . .

My first chilli bean that tasted like I was eating red-hot fire.
When I first held a five pound note.
My special mum, so I can have her all to myself.
A fireman's lift from a black, furry, gentle grizzly bear.

I will put in the box . . .

A piggyback from a muscly gorilla.
A lift home on the back of the beautiful, feathery falcon.

My box is made of lots of precious jewels
And has my initials in it.

I will put in the box . . .

Nothing more because the box is all the happy thoughts in my mind.

Jacob Kahan (10)
Grass Royal Junior School, Yeovil

The Magic Box

(Based on 'Magic Box' by Kit Wright)

I will put in the box . . .

My cat's first miaow in the big front room,
The first time I fell off my big horse
The first time my small puppy dog walked up the stairs.

I will put in the box . . .

The first chocolate birthday cake
The excitement like a cream stallion at Christmas
A key to open a fantasy world
My first friend, Caroline who I met in reception.

I will put in the box . . .

The memory of my friend's horse
The nerves that I had in a Year 3 test
The first word that my mum wrote in a book, 'Horsey'
A unicorn's horn which is full of memories of people and animals.

My box will be made out of glass that shines
And metal that glints
Its hinges are made out of a horse's shoulder blade.

Terri Samways (11)
Grass Royal Junior School, Yeovil

My Magic Box

(Based on 'Magic Box' by Kit Wright)

In this box I shall put . . .

A studded jewel from dew on a winter's morning
A rose as red as a model's lips
The sound of a star twinkling.

In this box I shall put . . .

A memory of a forgotten friendship
A piece of music that suggests a movement
A pleasant surprise for when it's opened.

In this box I shall put . . .

An antique lace woven from a web of a spider
A reminder of how life has changed
The smell of clear air flowing around.

This box has many moods
It may look normal, but somehow it's not
Come with me to a far off place
Where sadness does not exist.

All for now my secrets revealed
I shall do many things with this box
Lock it up
Keep it sealed.

Gemma Taylor (11)
Grass Royal Junior School, Yeovil

The Magic Box

(Based on 'Magic Box' by Kit Wright)

I will put in a box . . .

The smell of fish and chips
A growl of the scariest dog.

I will put in a box . . .

The strength of a wrestler
Answers for the test
Keys for any place built.

I will put in a box . . .

A sound of a sea dragon
The taste of delicious burgers
The sound of the ocean.

I will put in a box . . .

The best dream I ever had
The worst, darkest, blackest nightmare
The salt water from the beach.

I will put in a box . . .

The warmth of my embarrassment
The box will be made with silver and gold
And kept in a safe.

Joshua Brett (11)
Grass Royal Junior School, Yeovil

The Magic Box

(Based on 'Magic Box' by Kit Wright)

I will put in my mysterious box . . .

A dragon from the best bit of China
The tiniest sand from the Sahara.

I will put in my mysterious box . . .

My very first flight
And palm trees swaying in the breeze.

I will put in my mysterious box . . .

Man U's first World Cup
And Beckham's first goal.

I will put in my mysterious box . . .

My bear so deep in my heart
And the first Olympic flame.

And then to top that
It will be made out of Blackbeard's treasure
And the beard of Jack Sparrow.

Kristian White (11)
Grass Royal Junior School, Yeovil

The Magic Box

(Based on 'Magic Box' by Kit Wright)

I will put in my box . . .

A bright, golden wing to fly anywhere
And a feather from a golden eagle.

I will put in my box . . .

The sweet voice of my sister talking
And my sister's beaming smile.

I will put in my box . . .

A photograph of my grandad on Concorde
And a whole wing of an ancient dragon.

I will put in my box . . .

An eagle with sharp teeth
And a stripy tiger's long wings.

I will put in my box . . .

A shiny, silver key which will open everybody's secrets.

My box will be made out of gold, ice and glass
And I will keep it under the floorboards.

Aaron Neal (11)
Grass Royal Junior School, Yeovil

The Magic Box

(Based on 'Magic Box' by Kit Wright)

I will put in my box . . .

The memory of when I met my first best friend.

I will put in my box . . .

My white hamster, so that I will never forget him
And then I can see him all day long.

I will put in my box . . .

A monstrous family photo
With a really nice wooden frame.

I will put in my box . . .

The sound of the deep blue sea's waves roaring
And to catch a silver sparkling star in the sky.

I will put in my box . . .

A pet tiger
So I can always look into its golden eyes.

I will put in my box . . .

A unicorn's horn
So I could wish for anything I want, when I want.

My box is made out of
Real lilac, silk, real silver and gold
I will keep it high on my special shelf.

Siân Andrews (11)
Grass Royal Junior School, Yeovil

The Magic Box

(Based on 'Magic Box' by Kit Wright)

I will put in my box . . .

A rainbow to pull out on a rainy day
Forgotten memories that nobody cares
Swaying sunflowers in the Saturday sun.

I will put in my box . . .

For the world help, hope, honesty and courage to anyone
A healthy harvest to people that need it.

I will put in my box . . .

A jewelled cobweb in the frosty morning
A fire-breathing goldfish with shining scales
A spell-casting wizard's wand.

I will hide away in my box . . .

The kill of a flaming hell
The pain of a shark's tooth
The wickedness and evil of the land.

My box is created with the ashes of Mount Suvk
And the handle is a mould in silver-coloured platinum.

My box can grant any wishes
It can take me to the gorgeous Gambia
And give me my desires.

Matthew Bollen (11)
Grass Royal Junior School, Yeovil

Magic Box

(Based on 'Magic Box' by Kit Wright)

I will pull out of my box . . .

A gigantic bowl of toffee bonbons
A conversation with one of my fun, forgotten friends
And photographs of family in interesting places.

I will put out of my box . . .

A silky smooth unicorn
A winking wizard and a wicked witch
And dollars dancing all around.

I will put out of my box . . .

A flying saucer and an astronaught's suit
And my very own dolphin jumping through a hoop
Some more toffee bonbons, a very big scoop.

I will pull out of my box . . .

The sound of a jumping Jacuzzi on a winter's day
A mirror of beauty at the end of a hall
And diamond earrings shining in the silver light.

My box is fashioned from opal around the edge
It's green on the top, as green as a hedge
The hinges are made from gold galore
Open it now it won't become a chore, I can assure.

In my box I have a travel machine
If I say the magic words
It will take me there
Yes it will, it will, it will!

Lauren Green (11)
Grass Royal Junior School, Yeovil

The Magic Box

(Based on 'Magic Box' by Kit Wright)

I will put in the box . . .

Keys to a villa in summery Spain
Where I hope it'll never rain
And a dream of a marriage with a funky, fashionable footballer!

I will put in the box . . .

Memories of all my responsible relatives
An adorable, newborn, perfect, pretty puppy
And my own cheeky chocolate volcano.

I will put in the box . . .

Lots of languages that I can luckily learn
The Atomic Kitten gorgeous greatest hits CD
Also tickets to the Atomic Kitten's cool concert!

And a *good* score for my smiling SATs.

My box is manufactured from . . .

Silver, diamonds and sequins too
Also glass and flashing lights
So when I open the lid to take something out
The lights spin around.

I can swim with my box, run too
But I have to go now
I've got work to do!

Gemma Lawrence (10)
Grass Royal Junior School, Yeovil

My Magic Box

(Based on 'Magic Box' by Kit Wright)

I will pull out of my box . . .

A conversation with my great grandad
The calm Canary Islands as hot as ever
The posh keys to a fast Ferrari.

I will pull out of my box . . .

A big bulging house as big as a hovering jet
A drive in my car as fast as a Concorde
A surfboard that can surf seas and seas.

I will pull out of my box . . .

A sweet shop which has every single sweet
My great grandma who I've never seen before
A sighting of the famous inventor Thomas Edison.

My box has golden corners which can tell the future
An eye of an eagle in the middle.

I will store . . .

The best friend in the world
The prettiest snowflake in the world.

George Gulliford (10)
Grass Royal Junior School, Yeovil

Magic Box

(Based on 'Magic Box' by Kit Wright)

I will put in my box . . .

The golden gills of gillifine
The spiciness of a chicken korma
The smell of rhubarb and apple crumble.

I will lock away in my box . . .

The monster under my bed
The vicious volcanos
And the smell of my mum's perfume.

I will put in my box . . .

Elly the elephant
Five fantastic dino heads
And the ghosts at the town hall.

My box is decorated with . . .

Shiny shark skin
Gillifine gills
And sugar for the hinges
And it has a key.

Daniel Robinson (10)
Grass Royal Junior School, Yeovil

My Magic Box

(Based on 'Magic Box' by Kit Wright)

I take out of my box . . .

A unique unicorn on a purple field
The sweet smell of apple pie
Terrific tulips playing all day long.

I take out of my box . . .

A pleasant photo of my grandad and a conversation with him
A ginormous dancing tiger that tells the future
A magic garden that when you step inside you go into a fantasy.

I take out of my box . . .

A dancing dove in the sky
Peace all the way round the world
Rain trickling down the windows, drip, drip, drip.

I take out of my box . . .

A key to a villa in Morocco
Where I eat lots of cocoa
A pretty puppy playing in the sun.

Sparkling silver
Rusty gold hinges
My box is full of magical secrets
Tiger-striped wood from corner to corner.

I can go to magical places
Big or small
Any place at all.

Paula Wright (10)
Grass Royal Junior School, Yeovil

My Magic Box

(Based on 'Magic Box' by Kit Wright)

I shall place in my box . . .

Swishing seas of silver and gold
Memories of broken hearts
Icy cold raindrops splashing on the window.

I shall place in my box . . .

The chalky smell of crayons on a cold winter's day
The heat of a bonfire when night falls
The sizzling of sausages on a scalding stove.

I shall place in my box . . .

A sparkling strip of sunshine on a very sad day
A twinkle of hope when all is lost
Golden stars shining brightly to brighten up the night.

I shall place in my box . . .

A dive in a dazzling ocean
A ride on a golden ship
A stripe from a Lear jet.

My box is made of . . .

Gold, silver and ice stars covering the lid
Hinges of dragon's teeth
And forgotten souls hiding in corners.

In my box is . . .

Happiness, hope and joy
With love at the bottom
And tears of loved ones passed away.

Bobby Webb (11)
Grass Royal Junior School, Yeovil

My Magic Box

(Based on 'Magic Box' by Kit Wright)

In my box is . . .

The flashing hovercraft hovering over people
The Nimbus 2000 bellowing above the blowing clouds
And the sinking of the Titanic.

In my box is . . .

Mr Bean bending to a well in a deep, dark ditch,
Homer Simpson stuck to the sofa and glued to the TV
And a talking penguin having a good conversation.

In my box is . . .

The ice of a winter's day, its mists freezes in the air
The taste of a frost on a cold, crackling day
The birds stay in, no sound, just quiet, plain quiet.

In my box is . . .

A golden mask which takes you to Dream Land
A flying carpet zooming in the air, swishing and swaying
My mum kissing my bruise always making me better.

My box is made of gold with silver, razor-sharp edges
Making it stand out.

My box can shoot out a little fairy with a pink glow
Which makes the world bright
All it is, is
Love!

Callum Shortland (10)
Grass Royal Junior School, Yeovil

My Magic Box

(Based on 'Magic Box' by Kit Wright)

I will put in my box . . .

A football stadium with fresh, green grass
My own shiny, red motorbike
A company building as tall as can be.

I will put in my box . . .

A little puppy, cute as can be
My own tree house high above the ground
A room where darkening evil cannot go.

I will put in my box . . .

A remote control racing car, the fastest there can be
My own rock band to make a number one
A friend to play with when I'm down.

My box is made of . . .

Pure platinum, shiny as can be
The top is made of tiger skin, furry and soft
The hinges are pieces from the World Trade Centre
And protected by the good of the Holy Heavens.

Christopher Priddle (11)
Grass Royal Junior School, Yeovil

The Macaw

Flying through the trees.
Soft and gentle as it fought the trees.
Sharp, razor claws to get the prey.
Blazing brightly, coloured, powerful hooked beaks.
Large coloured tail, like a shining blue sky.
Eats the rock-hard nuts and seeds.

Sasha Bowen (10)
Heytesbury CE Primary School, Warminster

Elephant

I shove and nudge my way through all the many coloured bushes,
As I search for the nearest bye.
Keep on nudging and pushing,
Nudging and pushing,
You've really got to try and try.
This puzzling maze,
In and out all day.
Really gets on my nerves,
To find your way round and round,
You need to rummage . . .
To get to the most
Amazing,
Delightful,
Part of the forest.
Sparkling,
Dazzling,
Salty,
Water!

Eris Harland (10)
Heytesbury CE Primary School, Warminster

A Storm Of A Rainforest

Gusts of wind battle against the tumbling, solid rain.
Above the sky, high emergent trees.
The gusts of wind perform the waves of a green sea.
The canopy of animals wrap themselves in damp, soggy leaves,
Like someone is cuddling them.
In the understory the heavy leaves pour out themselves with tumbling,
Solid rain like a top going on for hours.
Deep down on the forest floor floods of tumbling,
Solid rain make rivers of towns.
Back above the great emergent trees.
Rumbling thunder makes its way as if a king was coming.

Sarah Hand (9)
Heytesbury CE Primary School, Warminster

The Gibbon Acrobat Of The Skies

Swinging gently from tree to tree in the canopy high, high up,
Swifter than everyone else,
Acrobat of the skies, that's me,
With my baby clinging on,
Acrobat of the skies, that's me.
My hugely stretched tail,
My giant fingers,
Acrobat of the skies, that's me,
Part of the canopy's circus,
Acrobat of the skies, that's me.
Every day I do the same swinging, agilely,
From tree to tree to the beautiful, starry nightfall,
Acrobat of the skies, that's me,
Leaping, leaping all around, like a ballerina in the giant trees,
Acrobat of the skies, that's me.
Swinging from hand to hand,
Acrobat of the skies, that's me,
Flying like a great, huge bird,
Acrobat of the skies, that's me.

Rebecca Newman (10)
Heytesbury CE Primary School, Warminster

The Blood-Lapping Vampire

D rip, drip, drip, dripping through the rainforest.
R azor-sharp glittering teeth ready to dig into the wound.
I n the rainforest, all seen is not well.
P erching in the air, ready to slice deep.
P assing by an eagle is where is stays licking up blood with it tongue.
I nto a cave with its leg, 'Time to have a feast,' it says, in its head.
N ow just a head is left, with eyeballs popping out of sockets.
G hostly, flying, screaming, loud with sharp wings, up and down . . .

Blood!

Kelly Ann Mitchell (10)
Heytesbury CE Primary School, Warminster

Rainforest

In the rainforest warmth turns to heat,
Hot turns to humid.
Day after day.
The beautiful music,
Writing a poem.
While the wind howls a soft way
Like a cat purring on your lap.
The sun fighting for life,
At the same time it's giving life.

The solar powered rainforest
Keeps everything in line.
The trees plant their legs
And hold their arms in place,
As the invisible thunder gets angry,
Then outraged.
Animals shelter from the rain
As if it were cold!

Seedlings burst out of their imprisoned cell
Fighting for life.
The blazing sun emerges through its surroundings
Making a patterned floor.

The touch of frost is no more.

The heat of the sun has begun.
The worlds have met technology,
Like thunder to the ground,
But not the rainforest.
The rainforest hides.
Shrinking,
Shrinking, like a bar of soap.
No one can grip it.
Rainforests are the future,
But will they have one?

Poppy Nicol (10)
Heytesbury CE Primary School, Warminster

Rainforest

I'm walking through the rainforest ground.
I see the canopy with monkeys swinging,
Frogs drinking from the leftover water.
I see trees, constant trees, everywhere I go.
The awful stench of elephant dung
And the dampness of the rainforest.
I feel as if I'm going to be eaten by a hungry leopard
That's sneaking up on me right now.

The storm has started, eruption in the rainforest.
I'm getting wet, really wet.
I can hear it endlessly tapping on my head.
I feel like I'm going to drown.
Lightning crashes from the sky.
It crashes down trees and gives me a huge fright.

The storm slowly ends and now it's time for the bats.
They rush out, thousands by the second,
Like a volcano erupting.
I really feel I want to go home, but I can't.
I see the sloth upside down,
The parrot squawking like a crowd of people.
The birds are drinking nectar, is it bitter or sweet?
The trees are being strangled by a strangler fig.
It eats away the inside and slowly, the tree dies.
I scream as I see a snake, it swallows an animal, whole.
I run off as fast as I can, with my head pounding, with worry.

I run into a spider's web and get bitten
By the most deadly.
It kills in about ten seconds,
So, what should I no now?

Emma Reade (9)
Heytesbury CE Primary School, Warminster

Rainforest

A damp rainforest,
The trees stretch their arms,
They put on their crowns
And wait for the plants and animals.
A hot rainforest,
Animals look for shelter,
So down they go,
Beneath the giants.
A rainy rainforest,
Life puts on their jackets,
Hides in their homes,
Or even alone.
A stormy rainforest,
I hear the wind rustle,
Leaves crackle,
See them rot.
A dark rainforest,
Trees stay awake,
Stand all night,
Never close their eyes,
Just watch and guard.
A hunted rainforest,
People capture the apes,
Scare away the chimps,
Cut the emergent kings.
'Clean it all . . . clean it!
It must be clean!'

Stephen Shuster (10)
Heytesbury CE Primary School, Warminster

Forest Life

Life.
A struggle to survive.
All is blackened.
It's a fight to the top.
The storm is upon us.
Seedlings drowning.
Roaring thunder,
Crashing lightning,
Striking trees,
Wherever they go.
Nutritious rain.
Sprouting higher,
Shooting higher.
Evening falls,
Monkeys munch,
Too small to be devoured.
Peace.
Perfect peace.
Growing taller, taller.

Morning comes.
I am a tree.
My growth is complete.
I can finally live.
Maybe I can't . . .
Trees all around sapped
By strangler figs.
While I have delicate
Blossoms,
Pink, blue, yellow, red.
Foods of the forest.
Grown on 'Safeways'.

Wild creatures strip trees
Of their bark,
To kill them.
Not me
I'm too useful.
Monkeys nest and eat
Flowers from me.
I like the rainforest.

Jasmine Kate Lindsay (10)
Heytesbury CE Primary School, Warminster

Who Am I?

I'm the king of the swingers
I fly rapidly through the trees.
We live in enormous groups,
Who am I?

I live in the shiny, glittering leaf-layer of the trees,
Like a huddle of penguins,
All squished up.
Who am I?

We're a bunch of bandits,
Shoplifting fruits from a shop of leaves,
All shiny and iridescent.
Who am I?

I live in the trees that circle the clouds,
Way up from the forest floor.
All camouflaged in among the leaves.
Who am I?

My fur's all silky and smooth,
Like a bearskin rug.
I go to bed feeling all snug.
Who am I?

Shana Lewis (9)
Heytesbury CE Primary School, Warminster

The Night Walk

I was as terrified as a spider.
A spider someone is going to stand on!
The trees were snowboards, stuck in the ground.
The sky had turned off, like a light bulb.
The moon had switched off its high source of light.
The leaves were leaping down from trees.
I was hearing the trees rustling their twig arms.
I could smell the burning fire
Reaching out its long fire tail.
I could see the silhouettes of gigantic brown trees.
I could smell the dark, misty smoke.
I could hear enormous dogs
Barking, like a roaring dinosaur.
I had finished and I was like a balloon,
Bouncing!

Matthew Bone (8)
Heytesbury CE Primary School, Warminster

Parrot

Flying through the trees
Just like the breeze,
Without a care.
Just the feeling
Of wind
Going through his hair.
Without a fear
Of being eaten
By a bear.
Goes back
To his nest
To have a rest.
This is nature
At its best.

Harry Howlett (9)
Heytesbury CE Primary School, Warminster

The Gibbon

It soars through the air like the flight of a missile
Its black, grubby hair almost coming alive
Tree to tree.
Branch to branch.
The restless gibbon swings and swings.

But when the dark, sparkly night comes
The gibbon builds its nest
Like a buzzing bee,
This way,
That way,
Getting all the leaves.

Then the orange, misty morning breaks
And the gibbon swings again . . .

Jamie McDougall (11)
Heytesbury CE Primary School, Warminster

Rainforest

As the large, grey elephant silently took a giant leap
And as it battered the forest floor,
It made a thump like thunder crashing into a tree.
As he sucked up a litre of dirty water
And sprayed it out again
It fluttered to a puddle of dung.
The parrot flies above, spreading its iridescent wings
It parachutes down where it's clear.
It tweets like a violin playing a beautiful sound.
It starts to take off, it flies higher and higher
And then it's flapping in the wavey wind.
The rainforest is a wonder to all the living animals
Who live, eat, die and drink there
If the rainforest dies, we die.

Lauren Pinnell (9)
Heytesbury CE Primary School, Warminster

The Scary Night

The light is like a switch turned to off.
It's cold and I'm alone.
I am worried.
Scared.
The trees are like arms.
I stepped in a bunch of leaves;
It's like some old, cackling witches.
I hear hooting.
It's time for me to walk through the woods.
I am petrified.
It's so dark!
It looks like another path to walk through.
I'm nearly there.
I get to the trees.
Relieved that I did it.
Glad.
Brave.
I am so pleased!

Rebecca Schofield (9)
Heytesbury CE Primary School, Warminster

The Things Found In A Deep Sea Diver's Pocket

Old fish bones,
Soggy seaweed,
Ancient, colourful stones,
Foreign money from Australia,
Old, shiny keys from the bottom of the sea,
An old ship that sank in a shipwreck,
A great, white tooth,
A white shark fin,
A part of a boat that sunk in a battle,
A part of an aeroplane's wing,
A piece of see-through glass.

Joel Hart (7)
Heytesbury CE Primary School, Warminster

The Terrifying Walk

The stars and moon glittering in the darkness.
The trees so dark you can only see their outlines.
Leaves are rustling in the wind.
A girl crying so loudly . . .
People walking and running everywhere.
Hands going this way and that way.
People so scared that they may die.
Girls and boys so nervous and frightened
That they might go the wrong way.
People running into others nearby.
Hands reaching out to grabbing leaves.
Outlines of different people's legs.
People hear rustling and rivers.
Late birds singing to each other.
The smelly smoke of the fire.
The air filled with smoke.
When we all get back.
We want to go again.
To the dark, scary path.
I was happy,
I was glad with myself,
I wanted to do it again!

Anabel Giessler (8)
Heytesbury CE Primary School, Warminster

Colour Is . . .

Purple is like a juicy plum,
Red is like fire, flapping in the wind,
White is like fallen snow on the ground,
Green is like the softest surface on the sea,
Gold is like the silky-soft sand.

Lottie Hedley-Harper (8)
Heytesbury CE Primary School, Warminster

The Only Bit Of Sunshine

Monkey scratching, elephants' trunks are
being sucked up by ignorant nutrients.
Leopards crawling, bugs creeping that's what
I see in the biy.

Lowland gorillas doing 'The Ketchup Song'.
I can see the macaws and parrots swaying in the
breeze. Branches guarding the biy with all their might.

Elephants mark the path to the biy,
camouflaged between the elegant flowers.
There's a whole lot of sunshine for us,
staying here for hours as we bathe in the hot,
hot sun.

Jessica Agate (9)
Heytesbury CE Primary School, Warminster

Colour Is . . .

Pink is like a rainbow,
Purple is like a beautiful lullaby,
Yellow is like the shining sun,
Black is like a juicy berry,
Gold is like a magnificent ghost.

Kiya Burgess (8)
Heytesbury CE Primary School, Warminster

Colour Is . . .

Black is like a galloping stallion,
Green is like the softest silk,
Purple is like a glistening diamond.

Red is like a dancing flame,
Blue is like the glistening sea,
Green is like a howling gale.

Jake Coward (7)
Heytesbury CE Primary School, Warminster

Seedling

A giant fell from his two titanic feet
To the delight of young seedlings
Who plant their roots in his legs of bark.
The seedlings fight to get to the bright light
Which gives energy and life.
Now they battle to reach the top
Only one left, just under the canopy it lives.
It starts feeling orchids growing on its giant arms
And other plants with pools of water
Homes for frogs and crabs.
The time has come for our titan to fall.
The wind was rough and fast.
The tree rocked and then there was an ear-splitting crack
And the tree fell with a shuddering creak.

Good for new seedlings
To reach the top!

That's how our rainforest works.

Heather Newman (10)
Heytesbury CE Primary School, Warminster

Water

The pond is calm,
Fish leaping, flapping,
Splashing all about,
Having fun all day long,
Frogs jumping.

Jelly belly flopping,
Fill it up, squatting all about,
Now frogs and fish,
Leap, splashing to bed,
That's what happens in the pond at day.

David White (9)
Holway Park Primary School, Taunton

Gutters

Rain bouncing
On the gutters
Pittering, pattering
Like a tiger pouncing
Splashing on the tiles, trickling
On the gutters
Like a rock smashing
On the beach
Going drip-drop
Like a balloon
Going pop
Rushing and hitting
Down and down
Until it goes
To the sewers
Back to
Be cleaned
So you can
Drink
So you
Can have
A nice, hot bath.

William Massingham (9)
Holway Park Primary School, Taunton

The Ocean Roaring

Water, water in the ocean, roaring,
Crashing, smashing,
Thumping, bumping,
Roaring like thunder,
Creatures getting washed far out
From shore, getting washed
Into a water twister.

Matthew Cross (8)
Holway Park Primary School, Taunton

What Can You Hear?

Water is a lovely thing
Ponds and rivers are so calm
Sometimes drops of rain
Make a brilliant sound
Pitter-pattering on the ground.
From the sea you can hear waves
Pounding and lapping
Every other one.

Max Salter (8)
Holway Park Primary School, Taunton

Swaying

Swishing, swaying through the sea
Fishes dancing happily.
Jumping up through the waves
And swimming through the sea.

Rushing down through rivers
Swimming really fast,
Swimming really slow
And get slow, slow, slower.

Rebecca Williams (8)
Holway Park Primary School, Taunton

Swimming Pool

Calm warm water goes in ears and mouths,
Slow when put in,
Lovely to swim in all day,
Splashes when people jump in,
Noise when people splash around,
Loud and quiet most of the day.

Rory Grant (8)
Holway Park Primary School, Taunton

Water

Water, water, everywhere, water all around,
Water in the sea
Water in the river
Water in the beach
Water in the rocks
Water crashing all around
Water thumping
Water in the lake
Water in the waves
Water all around.

Jordan Jones (8)
Holway Park Primary School, Taunton

The Starry Night

A silent night, a starry night,
The moon, shining bright,
The stars come out to guide your way,
Then they go and come back another day,
Soon the stars fade away,
Ready for the day,
A silent night, a starry night,
The moon, shining bright.

Pagan Ferguson (8)
Holway Park Primary School, Taunton

Water

Crashing and swishing at the beach
Let's go swimming in the sea.
Water, water flowing down
Down through the hills and the town.
Swimming, swimming in the sea
Now I can swim,
Come with me!

Rhiannon Swateridge (8)
Holway Park Primary School, Taunton

Fabulous Fair

At the fair you can hear
People talking, people walking,
Music bellowing in your ear,
Motors revving loud and clear.
Smell the oil burning as you walk past,
Doughnuts and burgers never seem to last,
Smoke and fumes fill the air,
Ride the roller coaster if you dare.
Lights are flickering,
Alarming shades of red,
Aqua-blue and ebony-black,
Fill the sky, looking back.

Grant Adams (11)
Holway Park Primary School, Taunton

Water Dropping Down

In the bath the water goes drop,
In the sink the water goes plop,
In the pond the water stays still,
Until the fish splash about.

When you're in a swimming pool
You swim and you feel something like waves,
When you're at the sea, it feels the same,
But when it's pouring down with rain,
You'll get soaked and it plops,
If you've got an umbrella, it drops
And you don't get wet.

Shannon Carp (9)
Holway Park Primary School, Taunton

Water Poem

Swaying, swishing
At the beach
Swirling on the rocks
Crashing at the sea.

Yellow sand on the beach
People in the sea
Laughing, joking
Whatever next . . . ?

I come out of my house
With rivers there flowing and flooding
With people everywhere
Hot weather in the air
And we go to the fair water rides there
It's time to get to the end of my poem
But welcome us everywhere.

Hannah Cook (9)
Holway Park Primary School, Taunton

Swaying

Swaying, swishing
Through the banks
Trickling down the moist
Pebbly bank.

Meandering through
The metal tanks
Making its way
Into the big, wide ocean.

Crashing on the rocks
Making a heavy thunderstorm
Yellow lightning that is bright
Making a very dark, dark night.

Joseph Coombes
Holway Park Primary School, Taunton

The Sea

The waves crash down on the beach,
All salty and blue,
Spreading on the sand and crawling to the rocks.

Sea horses jumping through the waves,
Galloping with their mighty hooves
Until they reach the shore.

Dolphins leaping in the deep,
Past ships and boats,
Through the icy lands
Till they reach their dream.

In the sea all blue and deep,
Where the animals live
And where they sleep
All year round, they're not disturbed
Nor found.

Amy Ward (7)
Holway Park Primary School, Taunton

Water

Water, water everywhere, water all around,
Water in rivers, twirling
Water splashing on the banks
Water in pipes, swishing through
Water to drink from the taps
Water in streams, twirling
Water on the hills, gushing down
Water in the seas, splashing, splashing.

Lauren Jones (8)
Holway Park Primary School, Taunton

Stormy Seas

Crashing on the rocks
Making them slippery smooth,
Rushing and gushing
Churning on the beach.

Rough and ready
Black and blue,
Sea horses jumping
To gallop away.

Seaweed swirling
Thunder began
Boom, bang
Splash, splosh.

The tide is turning
Around the rocks,
Leaving seaweed everywhere
Goodbye stormy seas.

Joshua Bartlett (8)
Holway Park Primary School, Taunton

Water

Swaying, swishing
At the sea
Swishing on the rocks
Crashing on the beach
Let's go swimming
In the sea
The waves are splashing
Everywhere on me
The water is playing with me
Then I come out of the sea
The water is not splashing on me.

Leah Musgrove (8)
Holway Park Primary School, Taunton

The Ocean

The ocean, all lovely,
The coral, lovely and bright,
Fish swishing and swaying,
The night so bright.

The seaweed green,
The whales big and jumping,
Waves like a rabbit,
Sea horses jumping low,
Clownfish are joking well.

Crabs snipping, snipping like they do,
Waves getting very smooth
And not rough
And being very gentle,
Then the ocean is calm,
It is night.

Phoebe Scarborough (8)
Holway Park Primary School, Taunton

I Am A Clown

I am a clown, I'm a jumping, leaping and jolly clown.
I am a colourful clown,
Running around all day
Running from February to May.
My favourite colours are blue, pink and yellow.
Tinkling backgrounds, sparkling clothes.
Big, puffy hats and magical black cats.
I'm speedy and *crazy,*
Jingling and ringing, dancing and singing.
The end of the circus, that's all for now.

Chloe Snell (8)
Holway Park Primary School, Taunton

Monkey World

I saw a monkey
It looked happy and well
Cheeky little monkey
Looking rather swell.

Sad little monkey
Sitting on a tree
Sad little monkey
Bored as can be.

Baby little monkey
Clinging on a swing
Baby little monkey
Doing his thing.

Sneeky little monkey
Playing I Spy
Baby little monkey
Says, 'Bye-bye.'

Marcus Alba (11)
Holway Park Primary School, Taunton

Stream

On the hill flowing down
Finely growing in the town.
Crashing down the waterfall,
Landing on the rocks so tall.

Slowly, creeping to the lake,
There, I saw a slimy snake!
On its journey to the sea
Would you like to come with me?

Dominic Walding (8)
Holway Park Primary School, Taunton

Water

Water splashing through the river
Water going down to the ocean
Water going to the dirty sea
Water going down to the reservoir
Water going back into the salty sea
Back into the ocean
Back into the reservoir
And over and over again.

Water splashing through the river
Water going down to the ocean
Water flowing to the dirty sea
Water seeping to the reservoir
Water going to the mucky river
Water going back into the salty sea
Back into the ocean
Back into the reservoir
And over and over *again!*
The water is not playing with me.

Claire Ryan (9)
Holway Park Primary School, Taunton

New Shoes

I am a person that loves to dance
In my new shoes so lovely and bright
I don't want them squishy
I don't want them smelly
I want them just right.

I like my new shoes, so crazy I dance
I like to groove in the lovely breeze
I get so hot and tired
My new shoes are just right.

Casey Harris (9)
Holway Park Primary School, Taunton

Fairground Fantastic

The lights are flashing,
Shades of scarlet, amber and glistening white,
There's bangs and crashes and thuds,
The sound of whirring
And the rides are twirling.

The prizes are on show,
As wooden rod in hand,
People dip into the water to fish them up,
Children scream, adults shout,
Loud music blares out.

The taste of sweets, the taste of smoke,
The click of a safety bar,
The ride's begun,
People scream as it swoops up high,
All around them are the stars and sky.

The music and the excitement goes on past ten,
The housing estate complains,
Hot dogs are munched and crisps are crunched,
The bumper cars are banging,
The Terminator's squeaking and clanging.

At last, prizes and camera in hand,
We leave the fair
And listen as the noises die away
And all we can see is a glimmer of light
Then - *night.*

Sally Alexander (11)
Holway Park Primary School, Taunton

Fair At Night

As the crack of night the music thumping.
Generators laugh as electric tickles them.
As I see the spark swoop over my head.
The money rattles in my pocket.

I hear screaming running through my ears.
See people up high.
Sizzling hot dogs.
Smell the doughnuts as your mouth waters.
Touch the rubber on the rides.

The people scream, *crash, bang, wallop.*
The dodgems rosy-red, star-white.
Flicker of a light.
So I say, 'Goodnight.'

Anthony Millar (10)
Holway Park Primary School, Taunton

Water, Water

Water, water, everywhere,
Water all around,
Water in taps,
Water splashing me,
Water in a water gun,
Water spraying everyone.

Water in streams,
Trickling over stones,
Water for the fish to swim,
Water in the bath,
Sloshing all around.

Darren Pring (8)
Holway Park Primary School, Taunton

At The Fair

The time has come,
The fair is here,
I'm walking down,
Getting nearer and nearer.

The loud music is pumping,
The bright lights are flashing,
As I approach the fair,
The crowds get bigger.

As I walk in,
The rides have started,
Some whirling and twirling,
I feel more excited,
As I look up at the rides,
My favourite one must be the Ferris wheel.

It spins and spins,
Making me feel dizzy,
I'm getting impatient,
Waiting and waiting.

Finally, it's stopped and it's my turn,
I get on the ride, not a worry at all.

As it starts, I close my eyes,
We start spinning round and round.

The seats vibrate, people are screaming,
It feels like I can touch the sky.

The ride slows down, I feel really sick,
I step off the ride and run for a drink.

I get a drink
And some food,
I think it's time,
I'll call it a night.

Serena Spiller (11)
Holway Park Primary School, Taunton

Water

Water in the stream
Water in the town
Water in the house
Water in the window sill
Water in the class
Water in the bath
Water in the swimming pool
Water in the beach
Water in the sink
Water in the grass
Water in the pond
Water in the seat
Water in the toilet
Water in the hair
Water in the park
Water, water, everywhere.

Ashley Carter (7)
Holway Park Primary School, Taunton

Water, Water

Water, water in the head
Water, water everywhere
Water, water in the sink
The water is everywhere.

Water, water splashing on the rocks
Lashing the air
Mashing the boat
Trashing the windows
Trashing the sails.

Harley Collard (9)
Holway Park Primary School, Taunton

Water

Water in the rocks
Water in the river
Water in the stream
Water in a caring way.

Water is a lovely thing
Water in the sea
Water in tunnels
That's what water is about.

Georgia Allen (7)
Holway Park Primary School, Taunton

The Enchanted Wood

When I wandered into the
Splendid wood one day,
I noticed a lovely unicorn,
Who seemed to want to play.

I spotted a magical fairy,
She had amazing powers,
Her transparent wings twinkled
Singing in the breeze,
Sprinkling fairy dust,
Drinking sparkling dew.

The fairy sprinkled silvery
Dust all over me,
Back I returned to my
Warm bedroom.

Was it a dream?
I wasn't sure . . .

Briony Smith (7)
Horsington CE Primary School, Templecombe

Dragon

An enormous, scaly dragon,
Flapped its wings,
As it flew over the happy village,
People swarmed to see him,
It swooped up and down,
Round and round,
Gobbling up all the people,
The full dragon flew back
To its underground lair.

Sam Fox (8)
Horsington CE Primary School, Templecombe

The Unique Unicorn

Pretty, sweet and colourful
A smooth, long tail,
A silky, shiny mane,
Galloping hooves,
A spiral horn,
Transparent, sparkling wings
Beating, as it leaps over
The glistening rainbow.

Jonti Allinson-Epps (8)
Horsington CE Primary School, Templecombe

Dragon

An enormous, smelly dragon
Lived in a damp cave.
The evil dragon
Flew over a charming village,
Beating its sparkling wings,
Puffing floating smoke,
With blinding fire
And it flew back to its dark lair.

Lewis Godfrey-Cuff (8)
Horsington CE Primary School, Templecombe

The Hero And The Monster

Flashing wings,
Slashing swords,
The hero and the monster.

Fire-breathing dragon,
Sparkling-faced prince,
The hero and the monster.

Sharp toothed,
Glittering teeth,
The hero and the monster.

Choking smoke,
Silver scales as shiny as a star,
The hero and the monster.

Luke Wagland (8)
Horsington CE Primary School, Templecombe

Fairies

Golden hair,
Sparkly shoes,
Magical wand,
Beautiful dress,
As small as a mouse,
Pretty and pink,
Lives in a bough of an old oak tree,
Glorious, transparent, glowing wings,
Fairy dust,
Making magical wishes,
When children appear,
Magical fairies disappear.

Olivia Clayton (8)
Horsington CE Primary School, Templecombe

Dragons

Rough and tough
Enough to kill.
Sly and slick,
Ready to kick.
Teeth as sharp as daggers,
Ugly and menacing,
Slimy and fierce,
Tall as a skyscraper,
Fire belching,
Smoke snorting,
Flapping its enormous wings,
Launching into the night sky.

James Antell (9)
Horsington CE Primary School, Templecombe

Dragon

A flying dragon
In the sky so high.

A lazy dragon
Would not fly at all.

A green dragon
Would glow in the dark.

An enormous dragon
Would breathe fire into the night.

The evil dragon
Would frighten all in sight!

Bethany Coffin (7)
Horsington CE Primary School, Templecombe

Fairies

Soft shoes,
Skin as soft as a petal,
Glistening gown,
As small as an eye,
Tinkling tiara,
Smells like a lily,
Colourful cheeks,
Lives in the enchanted wood,
As big as London,
Drinking dew,
Casting magic every minute,
Spraying stardust,
As light as a feather,
As beautiful as a rose,
Transparent wings,
Shining in the sunlight,
If only they existed!

Lucy Wingate (8)
Horsington CE Primary School, Templecombe

All About Dragons

A lazy dragon has bad manners,
Fire and smoke stream from its mouth,
Sharp teeth and a scaly body glint,
Its breath is smelly
It's as tall as a castle,
It's as wide as the world,
His lava-like fire kills everything,
His teeth are just like nails,
Fierce and dangerous
Is that fire-breathing dragon.

Toby Wagstaff (7)
Horsington CE Primary School, Templecombe

Magical Fairy

A magical fairy skipping around,
The toadstools in a ring,
In the sunny and shimmering light
Glamorous and pretty,
Like twinkling lights in the city.

A gorgeous fairy skipping around,
The beautiful tulips that sing,
Sparkling like an elf at night,
The enchanted trees
Are as sleek as silk.

A gleaming fairy skipping around,
The still stars that shine brightly,
Sly and slow little goblins
Appear at the dead of night,
Love to trick scared people out and about
Dancing in the moonlight.

Emma Mylan (8)
Horsington CE Primary School, Templecombe

Dragon

An enormous fire-breathing dragon
Slowly crept into the tiny village,
Its big feet tiptoed,
Its green scales glowed,
Its giant wings flapped,
Its fire was invisible,
As was its smoke.
Suddenly, there was burning fire
Coming from its huge mouth,
Destroying everything in sight.

Joe Miller (8)
Horsington CE Primary School, Templecombe

Dragons

Rocks! Rocks! On the wall
There's a scaly dragon
And it's going to make
The gigantic rocks fall.
Knights! Knights! On horse backs,
Charging towards their prey,
Heroic shields and deadly swords
And they're going to kill
The sleepy dragon.
Flap! Flap! Beat the ferocious dragon's wings,
Choking smoke and boiling fire,
The brave knights attack,
Green slime and hot breath.

Harry Coates (7)
Horsington CE Primary School, Templecombe

The Cave

There was once an old wizard,
With a long, white beard.
His companion was a black bat -
Both lived in a creepy cave.
The gloomy cave
Was full of scuttling spiders,
Potions, a cauldron and
Many ancient books.
Inside the secret books
Were thousands of mysterious spells
Waiting to be found.

Alex Harvey (8)
Horsington CE Primary School, Templecombe

The Door

(Based on 'The Door' by Miroslav Holub)

Go and open the door,
Maybe outside there's chatting seagulls,
A bright sun,
Or calling dolphins, jumping way up there.

Go and open the door,
Maybe there's sand, soft and warm,
Some umbrellas like rainbows,
Or even blue sky.

Go and open the door,
If there's enormous crabs with sharp claws,
At least there will be fresh food.

Go and open the door,
Even if there's only rain,
Or a thunderstorm with flashing lightning,
Go and open the door,
At least there'll be fresh air.

Rory Harrison (8)
Keevil CE Primary School, Trowbridge

Sense Poem

I wish I could taste
Some salty drink of seawater.

I wish I could smell
A gust of air floating by.

I wish I could touch
The very hot sun.

I wish I could hear
The rare call of a golden eagle.

I wish I could watch
A man step into some red-hot fire.

David Vick (8)
Keevil CE Primary School, Trowbridge

The D Zoo

We've got . . .

Drowsy ones
Dark ones
Dizzy ones
And
Dim ones.

Dry ones
Dull ones
Damp ones
And
Deadly ones.

Dirty ones
Diddy ones
Dusty ones
And
Dangerous ones.

And these are just a few
Of the different creatures
You can detect
At the 'D' zoo.

Ben Streeter (7)
Keevil CE Primary School, Trowbridge

George Is The Best!

George is a champion Manchester United football player.
George is a red ball waiting to be battered in the net of goals.
George is a scarlet flash, running in a blur.
George is a number ten with machinery legs.
George is a red phoenix, waiting to pounce on the ball.
George is a definite 1964 Manchester United star.

Daniel Streeter (10)
Keevil CE Primary School, Trowbridge

The Door

(Based on 'The Door' by Miroslav Holub)

Go and open the door,
Maybe there will be a sunset,
A smell of flowers,
A river with tropical fish in,
Or even shiny pebbles.

Go and open the door,
Maybe you will hear the birds singing,
A market,
A crowd of people

Go and open the door,
If there is a pack of wolves
There in the distance
They are only howling at the moon.

Go and open the door,
Even if there's only blue sky
Or the smell of food,
Carved wood,
Go and open the door,
At least there will be a golden sun.

Claire Harbour (8)
Keevil CE Primary School, Trowbridge

My Puppy Is . . .

My puppy is a fur ball, full of love.
My puppy is a kitten, ready to pounce.
My puppy is a cub, play fighting and biting.
My puppy is a sleeping panther, snoring softly.
My puppy is a beach ball bouncing beside me.
My puppy is a lion, yawning, her mouth guarded by huge teeth.
My puppy is a leopard, playing with her small, furry body.
My puppy is the sun, shining down, inviting children out to play.
I love my puppy!

Jessica Nurdin (10)
Keevil CE Primary School, Trowbridge

The Door
(Based on 'The Door' by Miroslav Holub)

Go and open the door,
Maybe there will be a jumping dolphin,
Or a beautiful island,
Tropical fish in the sea,
No danger around at all.

Go and open the door,
Maybe the beautiful island,
Will have magical flowers,
With a shiny blue river to swim in with the dolphins,
Squawking birds in the sky!

Go and open the door,
If there are jellyfish,
They will be swept away.

Go and open the door,
Even if there's only stars shining in the night,
Go and open the door,
At least there will be the sound of animals.

Donna Turner (8)
Keevil CE Primary School, Trowbridge

Foxes

A fox is a secret agent, cunning and sharp.
A fox is a robotic spring, jumping far.
A fox is Concorde, chasing the chickens in the hay.
A fox is a bread knife, killing its prey.
A fox is a super car, fast and big.
A fox is a digger, which can dig.
A fox is a cannonball, fast and lethal.
A fox is a dim light, dim and memoryless.
A fox is an iron bar, strong as a wall.
A fox is the best!

George Caine (8)
Keevil CE Primary School, Trowbridge

The Door

(Based on 'The Door' by Miroslav Holub)

Go and open the door,
Maybe there's a fading sun
And jumping gazelles.

Go and open the door,
Maybe there's vultures circling
And lumbering elephants.

Go and open the door,
If there's a stampede of buffaloes
They are on the horizon.

Go and open the door,
Even if there's only trees.
Go and open the door,
At least there'll be shade.

Jacob Case (7)
Keevil CE Primary School, Trowbridge

Magic Box

(Based on 'Magic Box' by Kit Wright)

I will put in my box . . .

A small sparkle of dust from a flower.
A petal from the sun.
A glittering chain from a tiny elf.

I will put in my box . . .

A fairy wearing soft, pink silk.
A happy pixie from a wishing star.
A small finger from a baby crying.

I will put in my box . . .

A blue, sparkling blade of grass.
A pretty peach rose thorn.
Ponies galloping across a sandy beach.

Clarissa Reid (8)
Keevil CE Primary School, Trowbridge

The P Zoo

We've got . . .

Pink ones
Pale ones
Plastic ones
And Pretty ones!

Prickly ones
Priceless ones
Poisonous ones
And
Pleasant ones!

Polite ones
Particular ones
Peaceful ones
And
Patient ones!

And this is just a peek
At the popular creatures
You can peruse at the perfect
'P' zoo!

Charlotte Richardson (8)
Keevil CE Primary School, Trowbridge

December

De log fires de Christmas choirs
De donkey for a surprise.
De water froze, de lovely rose
De holy child arrives.

De walk around de icy ground
De presents from de tree.
De mum and dad aren't so bad
So give them a surprise for tea.

Bertie Smith (10)
Keevil CE Primary School, Trowbridge

The G Zoo

We've got . . .

Green ones
Greek ones
Giant ones
And
Great ones.

Gold ones
Gloomy ones
Grand ones
And
German ones.

Grey ones
Greedy ones
Glad ones
And
Gentle ones.

And these are just
A group of the good
Creatures you can
Gaze at in the
Gorgeous 'G' zoo.

Joshua Dobson (8)
Keevil CE Primary School, Trowbridge

Tom

Tom is like a can of Coke, always super *cool!*
Tom is like an alien, acting like a ghoul.
Tom is like a plate of steel, always really tough.
Tom is like some sandpaper, often slightly rough.
But I can assure you, this is better than the rest,
Cos my friend Tom, is . . . the best!

William Locke (8)
Keevil CE Primary School, Trowbridge

My Magic Box

(Based on 'Magic Box' by Kit Wright)

I will put in my box . . .

Three jet-black horses with gleaming coats,
The flutter of a butterfly's wings
And the glide of a glamorous bird.

I will put in my box . . .

The feel of the calm river flowing,
The smell of blossom blooming
And the sound of an ancient clock ticking.

My box is made with . . .

Woven, golden strips of straw
And its hinges of lush, green grass,
With all that, a layer of frost.

Georgina Richardson (11)
Keevil CE Primary School, Trowbridge

Sense Poem

I wish I could taste
A wet scale.

I wish I could smell
The air floating by.

I wish I could touch
The bouncing ball of a boiling sun.

I wish I could hear
The spider's noise as he calls for his friend.

I wish I could look
At a big queen ant.

Luke Tyler (7)
Keevil CE Primary School, Trowbridge

The Four Seasons

Winter is . . .

Winter is the colour white, settling on the ground
Winter is a ball of snow, twirling round and round
Winter is a block of ice, falling from the sky
Winter is bitter cold, waiting for spring's cry
Winter is a great season, almighty and powerful
Winter is a frosty angel, graceful and wonderful.

Spring is . . .

Spring is the colour green, grabbing the biggest tree
Spring is a hummingbird, pecking off a flea
Spring is the beginning and no way near the end
Spring is the time for happiness and making a new friend
Spring is a first born baby, whining his first cry
Spring is a beautiful landscape, oh my, oh my, oh my.

Summer is . . .

Summer is the colour red, fading through the sky
Summer is the smell of raspberries, baked in a big pie
Summer is a time to relax, play with family
Summer is a time to be happy and amazingly smiley
Summer is sweltering and very, very hot
Summer is my favourite time, is it yours, or not?

Autumn is . . .

Autumn is the colour fading away very slow
Autumn is not my season that you definitely do know
Autumn is leaves dying and falling off the trees
Autumn is a lovely dinner, with lots of peas
Autumn is another season, just like the rest
Autumn is crying for a reason, not to be my best.

Sam Smith (9)
Keevil CE Primary School, Trowbridge

The Race To Get To Sleep, Part Two (A Parody)

(Inspired by Brian Patten)

They're set, they're ready, they're off!
Nipper's first to get all his fleas out of his collar.
Gnasher's slumbering behind.
Who's going to win this race?
Nipper's first in the bath.
Oh no, Mum's been splashed with water!
Nipper's got soap up his nose.
Here comes Gnasher, he's in the bath as well.
Gnasher's got soap in his ear.
Nipper's getting out of the bath.
Oh no, he's slipped on the railings.
Gnasher's out of the bath quite peacefully.
Even though Nipper's got a bump on his head, he's still carrying on.
Gnasher's got his clothes on.
But what's this? Nipper's been bitten by a cat.
This gives Gnasher an excellent chance to win.
But Nipper's still carrying on.
They're both in the lead.
Who's going to win?
What's this?
Gnasher's got a skunk in his bed.
He tries so hard to get it out.
Yes, he's done it.
They're both asleep.
It's Gnasher, it's Nipper, it's a draw.
Hang on a sec, Nipper's opened one eye.
He's asking Gnasher if he is asleep.
They're doing the same thing.
They're both disqualified.
It's the hardest race in the world.

Josh Baker (9)
Keevil CE Primary School, Trowbridge

Guinea Pig Scurry

Guinea pig scurry,
Guinea pig hurry.
Guinea pig smell,
Rabbits do as well.
Guinea pig walk,
Guinea pig don't talk.
Guinea pig lazy,
Guinea pig go crazy.

Thomas Meade (9)
Keevil CE Primary School, Trowbridge

My Mum

My mum is a tree in the ground , branching out a hand.
My mum is a cushion, soft and cuddly.
My mum is an alarm clock, set for the morning.
My mum is a medical kit, bandaging over my wounds.
My mum is a computer, full of knowledge.
I love my mum - she's the best!

Natasha Parsons (10)
Keevil CE Primary School, Trowbridge

The Railway Children

Get on the train, now we're leaving,
All the sirens went off in London,
We were evacuated,
I was scared,
We may never see our mum again,
She may be in pain,
I don't want to leave London,
It's my home,
Bang!

Isabel Breach (9)
Keevil CE Primary School, Trowbridge

My Magic Box

(Based on 'Magic Box' by Kit Wright)

I will put in the box . . .

Ten wishes with a magic sunset.
The feel of a puppy's soft fur.
Colours of flashing gold earrings.

I will put in the box . . .

A beautiful music player within a ruby-red rose.
The goldest petal of a sunflower
And the touch of a hand.

I will put in the box . . .

The slimy, silvery trail left by the slow snail.
A baby feeling the cat's warm fur.
Kind thoughts in every corner,
Soothing sound of the singing thrush.

I will put in the box . . .

People skating and sliding on the slippery ice.
Soft scoops of chocolate ice cream,
The smell of sausages sizzling in the pan.

I will put in the box . . .

Still gold glitter around the rim.
Pictures of ruby-red roses for the centre.
A warm feeling all over
As you hear the soothing sound of a purring cat.

Rebecca Tyler (10)
Keevil CE Primary School, Trowbridge

You

You!
Your hair is like a golden stream.
You!
Your eyes are like flowers.
You!
Your lips are like roses.
You!
Your teeth are as white as snow.
You!
Your skin is as soft as velvet.
You!
Your skill of drawing is fantastic.
You!
Your voice is as faint as the rain falling from the sky.
You!
Your nails are like diamonds.

Gemma Nurdin (9)
Keevil CE Primary School, Trowbridge

Countryside

Gloomy clouds cover
Countryside mountains and trees.
Foggy mist floats high.

The river moves slow
The boat rocks on the water.
The man gently rows.

The green, green grass grows.
View is extraordinary
Blue sky, hanging high.

Amy Bond (10)
Norton Fitzwarren CE VC Community School, Taunton

Life

Life is not fair.
Your face is a mess and so is your hair.
Like I care.

Life is not right.
All my make-up's running down my face making it look bright.
Like I care.

Life is not great.
When you think a boy likes you, but he really likes your mate.
Like I care.

Life is not cool.
When you shout that you rule, but all the boys shout
To you that you drool.
Like I care.

Life is fair.
Because I am a millionaire.
I really do care.

Olivia Pring (10)
Norton Fitzwarren CE VC Community School, Taunton

Alien

There was an alien from Mars,
Who ate lots of chocolate bars.
He flew into space,
In a car race
And he rushed to the finishing line.
His prize was a bottle of wine.
He flew back to Mars,
To eat some more bars,
So he could win more races,
To put a smile on his faces!

Robert Stewart (10)
Norton Fitzwarren CE VC Community School, Taunton

The Battle In Space

My heart pounds like a child bouncing on a bed,
10, 9, 8, 7, 6, 5, 4, 3, 2, 1!
We're off fighting.
The aliens are like dogs.
The pounding of machine guns floating through the air,
As if the creation of life was over
And the four leaf clover
Did not exist.
Maybe I have to exit to the Heavens
And that I will never visit the heavens of Earth again
And have to miss my wife give birth.
Then a clang
Like the midnight slangs of New York
Or the taste of pork on Sunday night
Like the birthday lights.

Josh Mattravers (10)
Norton Fitzwarren CE VC Community School, Taunton

Smelly Socks And Coco Pops

Smelly socks and Coco Pops
I think of them all day long
They say they make you big and strong
And your hair'll grow nice and long.
Smelly socks and Coco Pops
My parents think I'm sick
'Why don't you go out and have a kick
And annoy your brother Nick?'
Smelly socks and Coco Pops
My sister thinks I'm crazy
I'm not lazy
Just shut up Daisy.
I just love
Smelly socks and Coco Pops!

Kira Lamb (11)
Norton Fitzwarren CE VC Community School, Taunton

Water Buffalo

Big as a box
Stronger than ten people
Making the floor shake behind him
Skin as dry as a kettle
Horns sharp as a knife.

Lloyd Cotton (8)
Norton Fitzwarren CE VC Community School, Taunton

A Bubble River

A bubble river running calmly,
Like someone sleeping,
Bubbling like fish blowing,
Trees dangling in the water like giraffes drinking.
Children swimming like they are playing in the sea.
Dogs chasing balls like children playing tennis.

Ryan Hallett (10)
Norton Fitzwarren CE VC Community School, Taunton

Babies

When they are newborn, they are wrinkly,
Very much like elephant skin, they are crinkly.
A baby's nappy is pooey,
It also looks yellow and gooey.
A baby's voice can be like a drum,
Always calling for their mum.
But babies are best when at rest,
Sleeping and snoring upon my chest.

Alexander Izzard (9)
Parkfield Primary School, Taunton

Kittens

Having fun
Ties undone
In and out
Cute pout
Furry nose
Funny pose
Jump up
Chase the pup
Roll around
Squeaking sound
In a pocket
Like a rocket
Be ready
Go steady
Miaow
Pow wow
Under bed
Hit your head
Furry coats
Torn up notes
Like alarm
Bite your arm
Feline
Kitten whine
Go to sleep
Don't peep
Curl up
Like a cup
Goodnight
Turn out light.

Holly Ashford (10)
Parkfield Primary School, Taunton

Split Personalities

People try to get on with life
But it's easier said than done
If you have a split personality
How can you ever have fun?

Delighted, sad, calm or *mad!*
How can you choose who to be?
Life would be very strange indeed
With a split personality.

Monday - rough
Tuesday - tough
Wednesday - mean
Thursday - keen
Friday - sad
Saturday - bad
Sunday - who on earth shall I be?

Fat, thin
Brainy, dim
Plain, arty
Shy, tarty!
Smiling, glad
Behaving bad
Boyish, pink
It's hard to think!

What's the point in being *double?*
All it does is cause you *trouble!*

Ruby Kite (10)
Parkfield Primary School, Taunton

Heart

My heart is red
You make me feel free
You put all the bad things away.

But then you turn
It is black now
Bring all the bad things back.

I am confused
I don't know what happened
You make me weak, sad, helpless and lost.

You push me away
I have no place to go
I am in the streets
In a corner, crying.

Joshua Miller (10)
Parkfield Primary School, Taunton

Dogs

My dog likes to run in the park,
But there is a certain duck that is sure to make her bark.
She likes to chase a ball,
But then never comes when I call.

She chases a broom,
All around the room.
She loves to fetch a stick
And rewards me with a lick.

When Mum isn't looking she jumps on my bed
And I pretend she is my favourite ted.
We love to have a cuddle,
But the duvet gets in a muddle.

Emily Baker (10)
Parkfield Primary School, Taunton

Storms

Big storm
Early morn
Thunder crash
Lights flash
Trees swish
Cats hiss
Dogs bark
In the dark
Wind howls
Child yowls
Dad snores
Mouse gnaws
Pitch-black
Like a sack
Trees fall
Burst my ball
Getting worse
Like a curse.

Jasmine Ballardie (10)
Parkfield Primary School, Taunton

Santa Claus

S anta is coming,
A wake in bed,
N ot a moment to dread,
T ie my stocking to my bed,
A very nice man is Santa.

C ome on Santa, hurry up,
L ove comes with all his presents,
A wake still waiting for him,
U nder the covers going to sleep,
S anta is here.

Zoe Oliver (8)
Parkfield Primary School, Taunton

The Storms

Thunder
Blunder
Sky flash
Car crash
Rampage
Striking rage
All about
People shout
People cry
Oh my!
Stormy night
What a fright
Scared cops
Storm stops.

Andrew Beaumont (10)
Parkfield Primary School, Taunton

Weather

What is the weather on about?

Why is the tremor so suspiciously cunning?
Why is the fog like a curse from the Devil?
Why has the tornado got so much dynasty?

Why has the lightning got a reign of power?
Why is the thunder so full of stamina?
Why is the gale so vast and powerful?

Why has the sleet got an urge for vengeance?
Why is the rainbow so delightfully tropical?
Who does the weather think it is?

Aaron Macdonald (10)
Parkfield Primary School, Taunton

The Beast

When we opened the door yesterday
Beyond it we found
Something unique and fabulous
That left us spellbound . . .

When we opened the door
We found a beast
All brown and fearsome he looked
He wanted a feast.

He was very weird
We gave him some food
We greeted him
Which left him in a good mood.

He opened his hands
He gave us a toy
We asked him what he was
He said he was a boy.

He had sharp teeth
And spiky hair
He had sharp claws
And was as brown as a bear.

Joseph Brown (10)
Parkfield Primary School, Taunton

My Grandpa

G ives me pocket money every week
R eads me a bedtime story.
A lways helps me with my homework.
N ever lets me down.
D ozes off in front of the TV!
P roud of his family.
A nd I know he is the best.

Hannah Lucas (9)
Parkfield Primary School, Taunton

My Birthday

For my birthday, I want . . .

A dance mat,
A real life rat.
Loads of sweets
And different treats.
A big party,
Loads of Smarties.
A cuddly toy,
For a girl, not a boy.
A pet dog,
To chase a big log.
And best of all,
To own the mall!

Sophie Cox (10)
Parkfield Primary School, Taunton

Animals

Dogs are loud
Cats are proud.

Guinea pigs squeak
Fish can't speak.

Monkeys swing
Parrots have wings.

Lions roar
Bears snore.

Snakes bite
Tigers fight.

At night, they all sleep tight.

Abigail Stone (9)
Parkfield Primary School, Taunton

God!

Who is God?
Where is God?
Is He black,
Or is He white?
I don't know,
No one knows.

I wish I could see Him
Shake His hand and all
I would feel even more special
That I've shaken 'His' hand.

I wonder if He has a dog?
I wonder if He watches TV?
I wonder if He listens to music,
Or does He watch me?

I am special,
We are all special to God,
Who is God?
Where is God?
Nobody knows,
But one thing I know:
He loves me!

Emily Dunningham (10)
Parkfield Primary School, Taunton

Hot And Cold Seasons

Winter is like a frosty freezer,
Sapphire-blue ice crunching under my feet.
Snow as white as a fluffy cloud.

As hot as an oven in summer on high,
Sunflower seeds scattered on the baking hot floor.

Thomas Stevens (9)
Parkfield Primary School, Taunton

Summer Haikus

Summer is sunny,
Lots of dazzling hot beaches,
Lots of people play.

Plenty of sunshine,
Lots of blossom trees blooming,
Flowers growing high.

Little pups playing,
Rolling around on the ground,
Sweet little faces.

Rebecca Elies (9)
Parkfield Primary School, Taunton

On The Beach

Walking on the beach in the summer,
I see some children who shout and murmur,
Swimming through the rushing waves,
And searching the lonely caves,
Walking on the beach in the summer.

Walking on the beach in the winter,
It is not the same as before,
It is cold,
Well, that's what I was told,
I wish it was the summer.

Hannah Kemp (9)
Parkfield Primary School, Taunton

Haiku

A big, handsome dog
Growls and barks at the postman
Bites his la-de-da!

Ashley Lamb (10)
Parkfield Primary School, Taunton

First Day Of School

It's the first day of school,
First ever school day,
There's no one in the playground,
No one there to play.

The classroom is empty,
The blackboard is bare,
The teacher is gone,
I can't see a desk or chair.

The staffroom is silent,
Chairs put back,
Cold cups of coffee,
Turning dark black.

In the canteen,
Not a soul in sight,
Mashed potato on the floor,
Dinner ladies on strike?

Now I remembered,
What's the point of my seek?
The first day of school,
Starts next week!

Tess Gillham (10)
Parkfield Primary School, Taunton

The Pony

Flowing mane of inky-black,
Brushing across a chestnut brown back.
Galloping feet over meadow miles,
People watch over isolated stiles.

Neigh, neigh, the demanding call,
Galloping pony across the moor.
Rolling eyes, with pointed ears,
The pony who never fears.

Sophie Morgan (10)
Parkfield Primary School, Taunton

The Weather

What's the weather on about?
Why is the hurricane in a hurry to rip things in half?
Why does the tornado tear things in two?
Why is the mist so dark and damp?
Why is the sleet so slidy and slippery?
Why does the lightning lure us to cover?
Why does the gale gain things we own?
Why does the snowstorm scare us so much?
Why is the rainbow so fruity and tropical?
Why does the hail keep us hostage in houses?
Who does the weather think it is?

Robert Hayes (10)
Parkfield Primary School, Taunton

Summer Days

S ometimes summer is hot
U ntil the sun goes down
M um, my sunlotion ran out!
M um, I want a swim
E very minute really hot
R ed and sunburnt.

D ad said, 'It's time for a barbeque'
A nyway I'll get the stuff
Y eah, let's have a barbie
S ummer days are really fun.

Amy Howes (8)
Parkfield Primary School, Taunton

My Puppy

My pup
In cup
All around
Big pound
Ink spilt
On quilt
Bottles smash
Big crash
Barking
Larking
Up tree
With me
Lunchtime
All mine
Play over
Eating clover
Off light
Goodnight!

Ellie Kidsley (9)
Parkfield Primary School, Taunton

Dolphins

Splashing about in the sea
Now I can also see three
Sharp fins don't mistake them for sharks.
Gliding along like soft larks,
8000 reasons to like them,
Their rubbery skin is like a gem.

You should know by now what I'm talking about
I'm talking about *dolphins!*

Jamie-Lee Cosgree (8)
Parkfield Primary School, Taunton

Night Flight

Old stars and new stars shimmering above my earthly body,
The moon's silver light cast over this dreamy world.
I have a feeling of passion, strength and eagerness,
I want to float to this wondrous Heaven, beyond the stars.

I want to be free among these glorious galaxies,
Swimming through the spacious solar system.
Crashing comets collide with me,
The monstrous rays of sun lay their heat upon my shoulders.

I am a spaceship, through space I fly,
Round and round Saturn, up and over Mars.
Through the Milky Way, trailing through the stars,
Undiscovered planets I flutter pass.

My virtual space gets broken,
My dreamy spaceship lands with a crash.
For clouds now obscure my vision of joy
And my flight of fancy fades, for now.

Saffron Robertson (9)
Parkfield Primary School, Taunton

The Weather

What's the weather on about?
Why is the mist so mysterious?
Why does the gale blow things down?

Why does the tornado spin so fast?
Why is the lightning so harmful?
Why is the sleet such a tearaway?

Why is the rainbow so full of colours?
Why is the thunder so loud?
Who does the weather think it is?

Jonathan Limm (10)
Parkfield Primary School, Taunton

The Door

When we opened the door yesterday,
Beyond it we found
Something unique and fabulous
That left us spellbound.

A strange door covered in gold
Open in front of me
I see a solid gold castle
I find a gold key.

I step into this strange land
Suddenly I'm wearing a silky dress
My hair so golden, blows in the air
I know I'm a true guest.

A man riding a snowy-white horse
He climbed down and gently kissed my soft hand
The snowy horse was a unicorn with a gold horn
I love this enchanted place, it's the best land.

A flash of light appeared
I see something on my finger
He helped me on the beautiful unicorn
He took his helmet off, the king he was.

The fruits are all like rare rubies
The grass is like jade
The handsome king was making something
A golden crown for me, he made.

Kimberley McEvansoneya (10)
Parkfield Primary School, Taunton

There Was A Young Boy

There was a young boy who was eight
Who ran up a hill with his mate
But when he got up there
The wind blew his hair
He ran down at a terrible rate.

James Browning (8)
Parkfield Primary School, Taunton

Beach

Sunshine
All mine
Volleyball
Play for all
Lie down
Getting brown
Hot sun
Having fun
Sunbed
Getting red
Ice cream
In a dream
Lemonade
Bucket, spade
Rock pool
So cool
Eat a pie
Goodbye.

Lydia Murphy (10)
Parkfield Primary School, Taunton

The Snakes

T he snake goes around the jungle,
H e looks around evilly,
E ating every mouse.

S camp is his enemy,
N ever sharing,
A lways in a fight,
K illing the victim,
E ventually making friends,
S uddenly is nice.

Harriet Walsh (8)
Parkfield Primary School, Taunton

Winter

Snowballs
Icicles
Snowmen
Frozen
Slippy
Slushy
Bitter, bleak
I feel weak
Ice is numbing
Santa's coming
Christmas
Is a fuss
Presents
All sent
No school
That's cool
Time for bed
Rest my head
Christmas Day
Hooray
I get up
I've got a pup!

Bethan Rayner (10)
Parkfield Primary School, Taunton

Dan

One night as Dan went to bed,
He stumbled and broke his head,
'Ow!' he cried
'I have died!'
And he wished he wasn't dead!

Kelly York (10)
Parkfield Primary School, Taunton

Thin, Summer Poem

Hot sun
Having fun
Playing ball
Is cool
Summer wear
Deckchair
Ice cream
Sunbeam
Sun block
Wear frock
Lying down
Getting brown
Lemonade
Bucket, spade
Hot food
Good mood
In car
So far
Bye-bye
I cry.

Eleanor Roderick (9)
Parkfield Primary School, Taunton

Fear

Fear is like a black and grey mist lurking behind you.
Fear tastes like a puddle of mud lurking around.
Fear smells like the ashes bursting from a volcano.
Fear looks like the pain and sadness of a grave lying on the ground.
It sounds like the dark voices from beyond.
It feels like an abandoned street.

Russell Gilbert (10)
Parkfield Primary School, Taunton

Monkey

Monkey, a spirit in the tree,
Monkey, so agile.
He swallows a banana,
In one gulp.
He climbs a tree,
As fast as lightning.
Wherever he swings,
All animals move away.
He swings better than any man,
Young or old.
With his single tail,
He hangs on a branch.
If he had two tails,
He would not need arms or legs.

Michael Ying (10)
Parkfield Primary School, Taunton

Storms

Sky black
Thunder crack
Rain pours
Wet moors
Candles bright
All light
Cars crash
Lightning flash
People shout
All about
Wet puddles
All in muddles
Window clash
Lighting flash.

Amelia Salmon (10)
Parkfield Primary School, Taunton

Where All The Sounds Went

(Based on 'The Sound Collector' by Roger McGough)

A stranger called this morning
Dressed in black and white
Put all the sounds into a bag
And then took off for flight.

The sizzling of the sausages
The boiling of the egg
The tweeting of the birds
As it's running through your head.

The crackling of the crispies
The burning of the toast
The rustling of the trees
As they're swinging in the breeze.

The barking of the dogs
The sniffing of the hogs
The leaping of the frogs
As they're jumping on the logs.

A stranger called this morning
He didn't leave his name
And took all the sound away
Will life ever be the same?

Jessica Fryer-Sims (10)
Parkfield Primary School, Taunton

Grandads And Grandmas

Grandmas are so old
Grandads are so bald
Grandmas are so wobbly
Grandads are so knobbly
Grandmas are so tired
Grandads are retired
Grandmas are so scary
Grandads are so hairy.

Adam Salter (10)
Parkfield Primary School, Taunton

The Sound Collector

(Based on 'The Sound Collector' by Roger McGough)

'A stranger called this morning
Dressed all in black and grey
Put every sound in a bag
And carried them away'.

The tapping of the tabby cat
The brushing of a broom
The popping of the toaster
As I am cleaning the room.

The gnawing of the hamster
As I feed her food
The singing of the canary
As I get out of bed.

The sizzling of the bacon
The smell of burning toast
The steaming of the kettle
Are the things that I hate the most.

'A stranger called this morning
He didn't leave his name
Left us only silence
Life will never be the same'.

Georgina Trick (10)
Parkfield Primary School, Taunton

The Forest Monkey

The monkey roams the trees,
Looking for things to eat,
Their elegant feet help the
Monkey to leap.
They jump from tree to tree,
With their friends,
Right until the day ends.

Elliot Cook (11)
Parkfield Primary School, Taunton

All About The Sea

The sea, sea, sea, sea
I love the sea
Every day I want to go to the sea
I think the sea is fun
All day I can stay at the sea.

The sea, sea, sea, sea
I am going to the sea
I can relax all the time
You can't stop me!
My friends will be there
I love to have fun in the sea.

The sea, sea, sea, sea
I love to jump the waves
That come a-crashing round
My legs, it makes me shiver
With joy or is that just cold?

The sea, sea, sea, sea
It's time to say goodbye
I hope to come again
When the sun is shining.

Charlotte Upton (9)
Parkfield Primary School, Taunton

Emotion Poems

Happy looks like the yellow, beautiful sun,
Happy sounds like a football crowd cheering,
It tastes like warm crumble,
It smells like you've just bought chips,
It feels like you are on top of the football league.

Sadness looks like a grey cloud
It tastes like a sour apple,
Feels like you are going to be buried,
It smells like thick mud.

Daniel Cowans (10)
Parkfield Primary School, Taunton

The Headless Knight

Slash, ting, boom, boom, crack, crack
The headless knight screams through the night
Searching, screaming, slashing, pulverising,
Through the devilish night.

Black, dark, spooky, creepy, crazy
The headless knight, hungry for the taste of blood
Slurping, sizzling, scary,
Fighting with all his power
Through the devilish night.

Night-time drew in,
Thunder clouds formed,
The pounding of hooves on the forest floor,
Lightning flash revealing gruesome shadows
Through the devilish night.

Dawn breaks and the shadows lift
Birds singing musically
The world comes to life
And there's nothing left of the devilish night.

Duncan John Verwey (10)
Parkfield Primary School, Taunton

A Crocodile Poem

Lying patiently
His jaw ready to bite
Then he strikes, tearing its prey to shreds.

Fast killer
He lies in wait
Then hits them hard.

Elegant murderer
A loving kiss
As he breaks their bones.

David Brawn (10)
Parkfield Primary School, Taunton

Tennis

Game starts
Beating hearts
In the net
To regret
Ball boy runs
Try to stun
Hits the ball
Numbers call
Strong racket
To hack it
Points to score
People snore
Strawberries, cream
Grass so green
End the match
With great catch.

Ana-Maria Williams (10)
Parkfield Primary School, Taunton

The Pool

S till and calm the water in the pool
W hile no one dares to enter
I mmediately someone jumps in
M iles of ripples begin
M illing around the pool
I n the water, everyone splashing
N oises of enjoyment can be heard
G reat fun is had by all.

P eople jump in and out
O ut and in people swim
O ver the time people come and go
L ots of fun had by everyone.

Lucy White (9)
Parkfield Primary School, Taunton

Blossom

I walk outside wind blowing at my hair.
What do I see?
A blanket of blossom lying ahead.
What is that?
It can't be blossom, *no* not that big.
I shiver and quiver
I don't know what to do.
I run down the street
Not knowing where to go
Look over there, piled up,
A blanket of blossom in thin air.
I run back home
Standing there, was my dad
In blossom piled up to his knees.

Ashleigh Russell (8)
Parkfield Primary School, Taunton

Moon And Stars

Stars are shining in the sky
In the darkest moment of the night
Not a soul is here, it's quiet and still
And all the beauty of all the light.

If you look over that tree
Beyond the house, what a glorious sight
The stars are shining but higher than that
The moon is shining with all its might.

The moon and stars are shining bright
What a lovely sight to see
Them both shining high and nice
We saw it all, just you and me.

Emily Cooke (10)
Parkfield Primary School, Taunton

A Stranger Called This Morning

'A stranger called this morning
Dressed in black and grey
Put every sound into a bag
And carried them away.'

The sound of the arcades
The chinchilla nibbling
The bark of the husky
The noise of the jet plane.

The rev of the Subaru
The scrapping of the cat on my door
The noise of the PlayStation 2
The girl next door.

The bacon sizzling
The eggs cooking
The chips boiling
The burgers frying.

The pop of the fizzy drink
The football match I watch
The bike bell which rings
The flush of the toilets.

The sound of your mobile
The noise of the movies
The sound of me jumping on my bed
The whistle of the trees.

'A stranger called this morning
He didn't leave his name
Left us only silence
Life will never be the same!'

Darren Cooper (10)
Parkfield Primary School, Taunton

Dragon

It swoops low over valleys and trees,
Up in the sky, he is free.
No one to say no,
Or where to go,
His shining scales ripple in the breeze.

His smoky breath
And gleaming tail,
He takes slow and
Careful aim
And then he shoots
His spout of flame.

The dragon is as free as a bird,
Everyone knows his game,
When seeing villages and towns,
He will use his weapon, flame.

Laura Alison (10)
Parkfield Primary School, Taunton

The Weather

What is the weather on about?
Why is the hurricane so full of energy?
Why is the rainbow so full of colours?

Why does the sleet come down on us so smoothly?
Why is the fog so down on us?
Why is the tornado so full of twists?

Why is the mud so fond of our feet?
Why is the sleet so keen to upset us?
Who does the weather think it is?

Jordan Ireland (9)
Parkfield Primary School, Taunton

The Stripy Species

The happy, beautiful zebra,
Sits proudly in the grass,
He holds his head up to the sun
As time begins to pass.

He's stripy and he's graceful,
He's humble and he's thin
He has lovely, long, elegant legs
And a beautifully curvy chin.

He lazes underneath the sun
And admires his body all day,
He leaves his shelter, when the time comes
And eats his winning prey.

Sophie Groves (11)
Parkfield Primary School, Taunton

Emotions

Fear is like a huge bear waiting to pounce
It tastes like an ancient cabbage
It smells like a coffin with termites
It looks like a cold ball of fire
It sounds like rolling thunder and banging drums
It feels like a black widow spider.

Happiness is like a colourful butterfly
It tastes like a huge chocolate sundae
It smells like freshly cut grass
It looks like a peacock
It sounds like birds singing
It feels like silk.

Elliott Norman (9)
Parkfield Primary School, Taunton

Snow

Cold snow
Great show
White snowflakes
Frozen lakes
Icicles
More snow falls
Snowball fight
All is white
Snow attack
Down your back
Snow in eyes
Baby cries
Snowmen
Made ten
So much fun
With snow ton
Home I come
Now I'm numb
Warming drink
Take a wink
Goodnight
Snow flight.

Lydia Osborne (10)
Parkfield Primary School, Taunton

The White Rhino

The white rhino is like snow,
When he strikes,
It is a painful death,
He spends all day chomping on the grass,
But when you get to know him
He is really friendly.

Richard Frazer (10)
Parkfield Primary School, Taunton

The Haunted House

In Black Street you will see a house
And it is quiet as a mouse
When you open the door
You will see blood on the floor
There you will see a black cat
Who is owned by the witch who has a black hat
There are stairs that are big as a bear
And the kitchen is full of hair.

In the bathroom there is lots of slime
And it weirdly tastes of lime
And in the bedroom there is a lumpy bed
It will make your head red
And the family room has the scary parts
The monsters play human darts
In October you will die of thirst
Especially on the 31st

Bethany Power (9)
Parkfield Primary School, Taunton

Snake

Snake eye
Black as the dead of night
Snake eye, sharp as a Samurai's sword.

Snake
Slithering like a sniper
Snake injecting venom like the sniper's shot.

Snake tail
Swaying like the waves of the sea
Snake tail pointed like a needle.

The snake!

Rory Tomlinson (11)
Parkfield Primary School, Taunton

The Lion And The Giraffe

The startled giraffe looked up and saw,
The menacing sight of a lion's paw.
The kill was slick and very quick,
The lion ate it up, in just a tick.

And then the lion strolled away,
Full up until another day.
As the hyenas cleared the mess,
The body became less and less.

Then the flies began to feed,
The giraffe had satisfied their every need.
The sun bleached its bones white,
The animal's skeleton was such a sight.

Jack Turner (11)
Parkfield Primary School, Taunton

The Ship Of The Desert

I see you wander through the desert,
The cocoa-coloured camel,
Ill-tempered, grumpy, yet hardworking,
The ship of the desert.

The only shade is a wilted tree,
Floppy as an old rag doll,
The only water is inside your hump,
From last month, your supplies are low.

Eventually, you sight a pool of crystal water,
It attracts you like a magnet,
As you go over and have a drink,
You look back at the heartless desert.

Isabelle Mott (11)
Parkfield Primary School, Taunton

The Zebra

This zebra has a white
Body like a whiteboard
Her black stripes are
Like a blackboard.

She jumps around, a
Wild horse all day long
Her huge eyes are
Like humans' eyes.

They have excellent
Eyelashes, I think her
Hooves are like
Beautiful high-heeled shoes.

Sophie Hatchett (10)
Parkfield Primary School, Taunton

Frog In A Bog

There once was a frog,
That lived in a bog
And no one knew his name.
He would sit on a log and watch people jog,
They all looked the same.

When the sun went down,
The log turned around,
The frog tried to jog into the bog
And that was his claim to fame.

Nathan Wilson (8)
Parkfield Primary School, Taunton

Cheetah

The sophisticated spots of the cheetah
Can be found on the African plain.
They can also be found, lying on the ground,
Tucking in to a freshly caught gazelle.

As the cheetah warily watches
For any unwanted scavengers,
A leaf rustles, a twig breaks -
The cheetah pricks up her ears.

As quick as a flash
She leaps into a tree,
A ball of frightening fur, she snarls,
She strikes and scares the hyenas away.

Elspeth Rudd (11)
Parkfield Primary School, Taunton

Showdown

The rhinoceros has rough, grey skin
When danger threatens
He will protect his kin
He gets ready for the attacker
Positioning his head
Because soon the enemy will be dead.

He charges like a wild beast
Closing in for the feast
With one fatal blow
He defeated his foe
His enemy falls to the ground
Where he will never be found.

Tom Bates (11)
Parkfield Primary School, Taunton

Winter

It was very cold in winter,
When the snow fell on the ground,
I shivered and quivered,
When I saw what I had found.
It was a little snowman,
Sitting in the snow,
With a scarf and a hat
And a little carrot nose.

I took out the heater,
Which was warming up the shed,
I put it by the snowman
And off fell his head.
I tried to put it back,
But the body melted away,
Oh, how I wish he could
Come back and stay to play.

Lauren England (9)
Parkfield Primary School, Taunton

The Lion

He walks around
The jungle
His red, feather light coat
And his big bushy mane
Sways from side to side.
His mighty tail, flicking
When he hears a snap of a stick.

He goes up to the river
And stares at his rippling
Reflection, he stares into his
Big yellow eyes, he is proud
To be a lion.

James Barton (11)
Parkfield Primary School, Taunton

Light And Darkness

Light is like the sun,
Light is like a blazing campfire,
Light is like glistening tap water,
Light is like the swaying trees,
Light is like a cat or dog,
Light is like the summer's air,
Light is like a paradise,
Light is like a gold coin,
Light is like love,
Light is like the life in you and me.

Darkness is like the silver moon,
Darkness is like an empty room,
Darkness is like blindness,
Darkness is like the night sky,
Darkness is like sadness,
Darkness is like an empty stomach,
Darkness is like a backache,
Darkness is like a black hole,
Darkness is like the loss of your favourite thing
Darkness is like death.

Tobias Summerill (8)
Parkfield Primary School, Taunton

The Golden Lion

The lion walks slyly in the forest,
His sharp teeth waiting to bite into his prey.
His golden fur softly strokes past the trees.
Then he pounces like a kangaroo on its tea,
The deer cries in pain.

The lion's stomach is full,
As it sleeps to wait for the next day,
His wild mane strokes the blades of grass
And his tail flaps away.

Grant Whitear (11)
Parkfield Primary School, Taunton

The Grey Giant

The elderly elephant
Was wandering wild,
Plodding peacefully along,
Looking ahead at the carpet of green,
As the birds in the trees sing their song.

He eats the leaves -
From high in the trees,
His trunk is gracefully curving.
He settles to eat but does not eat meat
And gets up again, tail turning.

He gracefully walks,
Leaving footprints behind,
Making no sound at all.
Listens to parrots and to hawks,
Like a drifting leaf in the fall.

His shyness and quiet
And unusual diet,
As he wanders around in a group.
Listens to friends,
Then his happiness ends . . .

As he throws in the towel for good!

Robyn Kidsley (11)
Parkfield Primary School, Taunton

There Was A Young Boy

There was a young boy who was eight,
Who went out fishing with bait,
He caught one fish,
Put it on a dish
And then he met his mate.

Lindsay Knutt (8)
Parkfield Primary School, Taunton

Uh Oh! Trouble!

My mum and dad are snoring,
My baby sister's crying
And I'm in bed bored and sighing.
I'm wondering if I'll ever get sleep.
I've tried and I've tried counting sheep!
Then I heard a voice coming from the next room,
It was my baby sister's first word,
'Boom! Boom! Boom!'

Edith Humphries (8)
Parkfield Primary School, Taunton

My Friends

My best friend is Frankie,
We like to play with cats,
She came over for a sleepover
And showed me her toy bats.

My other friend is Chloe,
Who likes to play with me,
She found a big key,
But never let me see.

Hannah Frounks (8)
Parkfield Primary School, Taunton

My Dog, Henry

There is a dog called Henry who never had fleas
But when he went outside he caught a terrible breeze.
My dog likes to chew his bones,
He sits there all alone.
My dog likes to lick and lick
And chase after a really big stick.
My dog likes to go in the local rivers
But then afterwards, he shivers.

Georgia Davey (8)
Parkfield Primary School, Taunton

Subjects

Numeracy helps you with your adding.
Literacy helps you with your writing.
Science with experiments you can't forget.
Though PE is the best one you can think of yet.
History looking at what happened in the past.
Geography looking round the world so fast.
In art you have to use your imagination.
If the last one's DT, it must be creation!
Put all these things together and you get . . .
Subjects!

Sophie Knutt (9)
Parkfield Primary School, Taunton

Say Thank You

Say thank you to your family
Say thank you to your friends
Say thank you to life
And you'll have it again.
Say thank you to the Bible
Say thank you to your home
Pray to God and He'll give you:
A kangaroo
A pencil
A pirate crew
A glove
A king or two
A computer
A tutu
A queen
A toy called Boo
So what do you say?
Well OK.

Sarah Lanning (8)
Peasedown St John Primary School, Bath

Star

Little star in the midnight
Hoping each child has a
Wish of happiness, hope and dreams,
Making the night look more glowing
Than it seems
Make the night look brighter with
Your star teams.

Enjoy the day of life,
Look at the moon for hope
Your dream might be going down a
Snowy slope,
I hope your light can keep up with all
The hope.

Alice Graham (8)
Peasedown St John Primary School, Bath

The Vikings Are Coming!

The vicious Vikings are coming
The dragon ships are here
'Run away, run away,' the villagers all say
All the villagers run away
The vicious Vikings are here.

They'll steal all the money
They'll steal all the gold
They will burn down the city
They will burn down our houses
They will take all our food and water.

We'll have nowhere to live
We'll have nowhere to go
We'll be stranded out here, nowhere to go
The Vikings have left!
We'll build a new city
Then they'll come back, but we will be ready!

Stephen Gadd (8)
Portishead Primary School, Portishead

On Top And Under The Sea

I wish I could be under the sea.
But I had a change of mind.
There's too many sharks all roaming free.
But I would like to see some shipwrecks.
But some crabs might bite me.
It's all mysterious and dark.
Scaly fish all swimming around.
The wreckage of Atlantic City.
Where mermaids are known to roam around.

On top of the sea there are fishing boats.
Men are fishing with buckets by their sides.
Hoping to catch fish for their families.
Chucking nets into the sea.
What a nice place to be.
But all the storms and lightning.
Scare me out of my skin.
Lightning wrecking all our ships.
What a horrible place to be.

Jack Gradwell (8)
Portishead Primary School, Portishead

In Space

Once I dreamed about going to space,
To have a chat with an alien race,
As I used to lie at night,
Begging that I would be right.

But that was then and this is now,
I'm hiding from an alien row,
Alien ships flying everywhere,
One came two metres away,
It's not fair!

I saw the black eyes as big as a TV mouse,
I wish I was back at my old house,
I'll go back to my spaceship,
On the way, I'll try a flip!

I'm heading home,
But I'm still surrounded by the alien race,
I'm landing in Rome,
I've already met one face to face!

Ben Skipp (9)
Portishead Primary School, Portishead

The Rain, The Sun And The Wind

The wind rustles through my hair,
Swish, swash, swish, swash,
The wind cools me down,
Blow, blow, blow, blow,
The wind rustles the trees,
Rustle, rustle, rustle, rustle,
The winter wind has come.

The raindrops dribble down my face,
Whee, plop, whee, plop,
The rain sparkles and shines,
Sparkle, shine, sparkle, shine,
The rain plops into puddles and streams,
Splash, splish, splash, splish,
The whole year rain is here.

The sun keeps me warm and hot,
Phew, phew, phew, phew,
The sun shines down on me,
Shine, glare, shine, glare,
The sun makes sunny days,
'Let's go to the beach, let's go to the beach!'
The summer sun has arrived!

Olivia Pointon (8)
Portishead Primary School, Portishead

Someone Leaving

She's leaving!
I came into the classroom
And she said,
'I'm leaving on Wednesday.'

I will miss her being slow
I will be so sad, I might never see her again
I will miss her laugh
I will miss her playing with me.

She's leaving!
I came into the classroom
And she said,
'I'm leaving on Wednesday.'

I was so shocked
I was so tearful
I felt so weird
I felt I would never see her again.

She's leaving
I came into the classroom
And she said,
'I'm leaving on Wednesday.'

I'm so going to miss her!

Kennedy Marlow (8)
Portishead Primary School, Portishead

Friends

Friends are lovely things.
They cheer you up when you are down.
Friends are nice!
Friends are caring.
I love having friends.

Friends are cool.
Friends will share.
Friends are excellent.
Friends hang out with you.
I love having friends.

Friends are loving.
Friends are super.
Friends will care for you.
Friends are nice to you.
I love having friends.

Friends are lovely things.
They cheer you up when you are down.
Friends are nice.
Friends are caring.
I love having friends.

Leah Sperring (8)
Portishead Primary School, Portishead

My Unicorn

My unicorn is creamy white,
She's soft and snugly too,
Her fluttering wings make her fly,
She has got white, soft fur too,
She is the best unicorn ever.

She'll fly by your window,
That's very high,
She will go fluttering calmly by,
She will be high in the sky,
She is the best unicorn ever.

When she comes by and you're sad,
She will help you, hooray, hooray,
She loves to play,
She's never, never bad,
She is the best unicorn ever.

She has magical powers,
They lie within their bodies,
The white fur on her chin,
She has some magic flowers,
She is the best unicorn ever.

Freya Park (7)
Portishead Primary School, Portishead

Water

Water falls from the sky,
As a drop.
Water runs through the stream,
As a trickle.
Water flows through the sea,
As a wave.
We need water
And that is that.

There is only a small amount of water,
But we all need it.
Water can be hot or cold,
But we all need it.
Clear water is not always clean water,
But we all need it.
We need water
And that is that.

Different countries need water too,
Water, water.
Poor people only get a little bit of water,
Water, water.
The way of water is the way of the world,
Water, water.
We need water
And that is that.

Hannah Sampson (9)
Portishead Primary School, Portishead

Christmas Eve

It was the day before Christmas Day,
It was getting darker,
All the children around the street went to bed,
There was just one child awake,
Lucy was waiting for it to snow,
Then it started snowing,
Lucy heard a clatter on the roof
And *then* she knew,
It was Santa!

Lucy ran downstairs to tell her parents,
Then Lucy's parents ran upstairs,
Then they were shocked to see,
Santa Claus!
They stared and stared for hours,
They just couldn't believe their eyes!

Then it was Christmas Day,
Lucy had loads of presents,
Then she opened them,
Lucy loved all of them,
Lucy looked out of the window,
It had snowed heavily,
Lucy ran outside,
She thought it wasn't cold,
She threw the snow into snowballs,
Then she made a snowman,
Then it got to the end of the day,
Lucy loved Christmas Day.

Rebecca Young (9)
Portishead Primary School, Portishead

School Day

Children in school,
Children work,
Being kind children,
Children using white boards,
Children go out to play.

Children do history,
Children do the Vikings,
They work and work all day long,
They still work.

Children do competitions,
Children make posters,
Children bring in things,
Like books, puzzles and all sorts.

Children like to play,
Children have friends to play with,
Children have fun together,
Children go and play rough games.

I love school!

Poppy Manning (8)
Portishead Primary School, Portishead

The Year

Spring is so bouncy and prancy
When all the lambs are born
The birds are all singing
Spring is so much fun!

Summer is so hot and dry
All lambs are growing up
All the birds are singing still
Summer is so much fun!

Autumn is getting colder
Picking blackberries from bushes
Colourful leaves falling, one, two and three
Autumn is so much fun!

Winter is coming, getting even colder
Making snowmen out of freezing snow and ice
Snowflakes falling as well
Winter is so much fun!

The year is full of colourful things -
Like snowflakes, fish and the sun
The year is so beautiful
The year is so much fun!

Helen Trueman (7)
Portishead Primary School, Portishead

How To Train Your Dog!

A mouse,
Can live in a house,
Or outside,
Where it can hide.

If you get one as a pet,
I will give you a bet,
They will send tingles down your spine,
So you say to your brothers, 'No they're mine.'

A cat,
Can sit on a mat,
Or on a bed,
(It's too big for your head.)

But if a cat sees a mouse,
(In the house,)
Its mouth will go snap,
And catch that little mousy chap.

A dog,
Can laze on a log,
Or in the garden,
Where behind a bush it might say *'Pardon.'*

So, if you have a dog next door,
Creep around quietly on the floor.
Then make him come bounding through the trees,
To play with the little squeaky cheese.

Now tie the toy to the cat,
The dog will say, 'Now, fancy that!
A pretty little cat for me to chase!'

Bark, miaow, miaow, bark,
Off they run into the dark,
The next moment, it goes quiet,
If the dog catches the cat, he might fry it.

And so I end the story now,
To let the main characters give a *bow, wow, wow!*

Emma Hopkins (10)
Portishead Primary School, Portishead

Tyrannosaurus

Tyrannosaurus - he's stomping here and there like a big warrior,
He's got scaly skin and a ferocious grin,
He's got a big fat smile and a huge meat pile,
Volcanic acid leaking out of volcanoes,
This is the end of the dinosaurs.

Tyrannosaurus, king of the dinosaurs,
Lord of the beasts,
Don't blame me but he's had lots of feasts,
The killer mean machine,
He's very scary and very mean,
Volcanic acid leaking out of volcanoes,
This is the end of the dinosaurs.

The dinosaurs are dead,
Their bones are crushed,
That was the end of the dinosaurs.

Joel Hopkins (8)
Portishead Primary School, Portishead

Untitled

Oh, what a lovely garden, it must be, it must be
The scattering of the butterfly,
The baby dear cries for her mum
The fidgeting of the bungee-jumping bunnies
The excitement of water going drop, drop, drop
The trickling of a stream
The roses red, ripe,
The scent of them
Their lovely movement to and fro
The wind going through the branches
Swifting, staring at me
Tweeting birds
Leaves dancing along the ground
I open the door to the secret garden and I see . . .

Charlotte Millard (11)
Priddy Primary School, Wells

My Secret Garden

I opened the door . . .
It was a dream come true!
The garden was full of enchantment.
It was magnificent!
Immediately, I saw such a beautiful unicorn . . .
He crept towards me . . .
He whispered,
'Come with me, come and have a ride!
What could I say?
I said, *'Yes!'*
The unicorn would make my wish come true.
As soon as I was ready,
He took a leaping jump and *shot* off!
I wished that I could have wings.
Immediately,
I felt a funny feeling
Under my armpits . . .
And wings started to form!
I flew to fairyland,
A dream come true.

Poppy River (8)
Priddy Primary School, Wells

The Garden Of Rhymes

The old, dangerous door,
When you open it you will see further more,
Down the tunnel of walking willows,
Through the tricky twigs, that are not like pillows,
And all the frogs have hopping habits,
And also have the rabbits,
All you could hear was the robin and wind,
With rubbish that has all been binned.

Jason Griffiths (10)
Priddy Primary School, Wells

The Mist Of The Secret Garden

Shhhhh!

Open the secret door.
Find something you have never seen before!
You will have to look very carefully,
So be quite quiet . . . sh-shh-shhh!

Open the arched doorway,
With the creeping, crawling ivy,
Tangling up the wall.
Everything is quite quiet . . . sh-shh-shhh!

Except for the crusty, brown leaves,
Crackling as you step on them.
Crunch, crunch, crunch.

Up the old, hard steps . . .
You come across an ancient, frozen statue.
It makes you stop and stare.

The mist is everywhere . . .
Swirl, swirll, swirlll.
The cold air brushes against your cheeks.
You walk on until you see a spot of life.
All of a sudden, you know the garden is . . .
Alive!

Birds collecting twigs for their nest,
So spring is on its way.
As you walk over twickling twigs.
Crickle, crackle.

You come to a magic, misty pond.
You can hear water trickling down rocks . . .
And you come into not just mist - magic mist!
Abracadabra!

It's time to go back through the misty door
And you've gone . . .
Into the mists of time . . .
Tick-tock tick!

Hannah Edwards (8)
Priddy Primary School, Wells

Spin A Yarn

Enter the gardens!
Mysterious mist.
The trippy tree roots too.
The rustling weeds,
The overgrown plants
And the wrestling rocks,
The crunchy stones make holes in your socks.

The slippy snow might hurt
If you slip.
See a still statue!
A mansion house,
Ivy is all around it.
The windows are dark.

Go into the house,
See a table
With food piled high on top.
(Don't eat it! It is poisonous!)

Walk on
And up some stair
And you come
Face to face with a door . . .

Walk in and see a ladder
Leading up to an open trapdoor.
Climb up and
See a little black thing
With a spinning wheel,
Spinning incredibly fast!
Spinning and twirling its tale!

Gregory Mantingh (8)
Priddy Primary School, Wells

Secrets Of The Garden

When you open the door,
You see
Tripping twigs.

Go over the tripping twigs,
You see
Mysterious mist.

Go through the mysterious mist,
And you will see
Sleeping statues.

Underneath the
Weeping weeds
You will find
Growing growth.
The old, swinging swing
That's left on an old tree branch,
But it is forced to swing
By the singing wind.

Henry Peacock (7)
Priddy Primary School, Wells

The Secret Garden

The old, dangerous door
When you open it you will see further more
Down a tunnel of walking willows
The twigs and sticks are not like pillows
And all the rabbits have hopping habits.

Chad Millard (8)
Priddy Primary School, Wells

Secret Garden

When you open the door
You will see what no one has seen before . . .
Mysterious mist,
Smelling smoke,
Crackling, orange fire.
Motionless plants,
Trickling fountain,
Wintry wonderland.

Cold, shivering rocks!
Green, twirling ivy,
Brown rustling leaves,
White, frosty grass,
Flittering birds,
Snow catching everything.

Ford Collier (7)
Priddy Primary School, Wells

The Tiger Adventure

I'm going into a grey hut,
I'm opening the door,
I see four tiger cubs
Wild as can be!
I pick one up,
I'm stroking it
And soon it falls asleep.
I call the tiger, John.

David Sparkes (8)
Priddy Primary School, Wells

Crystal Bear

Soft, cuddly and fluffy, just like a cloud.
When I'm sad Crystal makes me happy and warm.
She has gentle, hazel eyes and honey-coloured fur.
She smells really fresh, just like my mum's laundry.
Crystal is an amazing bear
Because she's mine!

Hannah Langley & Jade Dix (9)
St Julian's Primary School, Bath

Snow

Delicious snow
United with the freezing wind.
Plates of warm food,
Hot chocolate too.
Mugs of boiling tea
To warm me up.
Ready to go back in the snow
And have another snowball fight.

Victoria Isaac (9)
St Julian's Primary School, Bath

The Sea

As I walk across the seashore with a gentle breeze flowing by me,
As the sun slowly sets.
I steadily walk over to the rock pools.
I find a little crab struggling to get out of his shell.
I help him.
He plods over to the edge of the sea
And we wave goodbye.

Molly Austin (9) & Aimee Horler (11)
St Julian's Primary School, Bath

Snow

Twinkling crystals
Falling from the
Frozen sky.
Frozen flakes
Of endless joy.
Icicles like
Sharp, gleaming
Knives.
Boiling winter coats
Like roasting beef.
When it melts
Running rivers
Of sparkling
Water appear.

James Kruk (11)
St Julian's Primary School, Bath

The Sea

Sparkling,
Turquoise,
Shining in the golden sun,
Lapping at the sand,
Seeping back again.

Swirling at ankles,
An invitation
Into the cool, refreshing serenity.

White stallions galloping,
Blue and bright as sapphires,
Leading souls into its depths.

Hannah Beswick (11)
St Julian's Primary School, Bath

Falcon

Sleek, golden plumage,
With a darkened breast.
Wings soaring, feet snapping,
Grabbing at unwary prey.
A shriek fills the air, loud and harsh,
Echoing around the mountain's peak.
Gliding through the marsh.
A field mouse hurtles for cover, lungs pounding with fear,
But this sudden dash for cover is too late,
Oh dear.
Those golden talons,
A symbol of death,
Have pierced the mouse's heart.
A rush of air and a beating of wings,
The falcon is in flight.
A severe and deadly enemy,
To all who are seen during the night.

Ellie Dimond (10)
St Julian's Primary School, Bath

Snow

Twinkling
Crystals falling from the icy, white sky
Frozen flakes of joy
Icicles like gleaming knives
Falling from the rooftops
Winter coats like boiling roast beef
But when it melts
My happiness goes with it.

Conor Ogilvie-Davidson (10)
St Julian's Primary School, Bath

The Ocean

Like gushing white horses,
Storming up the beach,
Lapping at the shore.

Bathed in golden light,
It glints like a vast, treasured jewel,
Not to be lost.

Covers the Earth, reflecting light,
Taking you to another land,
Far away.

Calling, inviting,
Trapping souls in its depths,
Swallowing them, then moving on,
Mysterious and undiscovered.

Jessica Wheeler (11)
St Julian's Primary School, Bath

The Sea

Clashing waves,
Sparkling reefs,
As the black night falls,
The waves clap their hands,
Relaxing in tranquility.

Carmelita Sanchez & Stephanie Jones (10)
St Julian's Primary School, Bath

The Sea

The sea is turquoise and reflects the sun
The raging waves go up and down
The tide comes to visit and then goes away
The salty taste is all around the turquoise sea.

Dominique Bedoya (11)
St Julian's Primary School, Bath

Red Pepper, My Teddy Bear!

Warm
Cosy
By a fire
Soft and furry
Like a blanket
Red as pepper
And eyes that
Shine as blue as the water
My teddy makes me feel
Happy when I'm sad.
Red Pepper's nose
Is as black as the night sky
He smells like my bed
But also smells like my mum's perfume
Really bad!
But best of all
Red Pepper's my teddy!

Serafina Collier (10)
St Julian's Primary School, Bath

The Sea

Shimmering,
Reflecting
The sun's golden rays
As it shines.
Throughout the long, hot day
Fish are flipping,
Gently moving across the mirror-like sea.
And as the sun sets,
My soul goes out with the tide.

Chloe Chedgy (10)
St Julian's Primary School, Bath

Water And Its Importance

Running water,
Dashing streams.
Crawling down the windowpanes,
Watering the trees.

The oceans filling,
Two thirds of Earth.
The surfers coming to the shore,
To surf the clashing waves.
The water clamping round their ankles,
To drag them out to sea.

The boats that cut clean through the water,
We're polluting all the time.
Why should we destroy it,
When it helps us to survive?

Sam Draper (10)
St Julian's Primary School, Bath

Silver Snake

There we see the silver snake,
Slithering through the night,
Slowly creeping by the lake,
Giving his prey a fright.

Coming into a new day,
Not stopping to look at the view,
He would only stop to look for prey,
The odd mouse will usually do.

Slowly crawling to the nest,
To have a well earned rest,
Not disturbed by a Fiesta,
To enjoy a calm siesta.

Ben Sutton (10)
St Julian's Primary School, Bath

The Sun

A giant light bulb,
A fuming ball of fire and
Flames,
A star shining bright.
A light,
A clock,
A guide.

Oliver McGill (10)
St Julian's Primary School, Bath

A Baby Elephant

His ears are like two big, rough melons.
His trunk is like a grey leather rope hanging from his face.
His tusks are like hard marble with a point on the end.
His body is like a grey boulder.
His legs are like grey moving trees
And his tail is like a long piece of string with a fur ball on the
end of it.

Abigail Burfield (10)
St Julian's Primary School, Bath

War

Guns are firing
People are dying
Air raids are warning
Planes are flying
Children are hiding
Anywhere they can find
Tanks are roaring through the streets
They aren't being very kind.

Matthew Dawson (8)
The Minster CE Primary School, Warminster

The Canal

Swans silhouetted,
Wing feathers ruffling,
Silent, synchronized drifters,
Buskers dabbling and dipping.
Their necks break ripple glitter
And ladder the water.
Professional performers dancing
On a darkened stage,
The Nessie necks,
Fishing for weeds.

Canal boats sleep,
Slotted and slanted,
Glued into place
Like a deck of cards.
Lying in the shadows
Straight and still,
Strung with fairy lights,
Endlessly twinkling,
Welcoming jewels of the night.

Lights acidic in the cold, dark night,
A lost treasure,
Fading away into the darkness.
A black cloud that time had snatched,
Like sodden dark robes.
Scattered, gleaming stars,
Fluorescing neon gods,
A lonely abandoned
Gently smoking
Murky river,
Meandering into a distant future.

Camilla Batchelor (10)
The Minster CE Primary School, Warminster

Night

He silently sweeps across the valley,
Veiling the sun under his black cloak,
Eyes shining like erupting volcanoes,
Searching for someone to surprise.

Ghostly in the inky sky,
He swoops and pounces on a lonely child,
Muttering his nightmare curse he steals away,
But as he lurks in the shadows,
>   The sun escapes,
>   Day has won,
>   Night has gone.

Jayne Goater (11)
The Minster CE Primary School, Warminster

Peace

If the world had peace
We'd have no troubles,
If the world had peace
We'd all have friends,
If the world had peace
We'd all care for each other,
If only the world had peace.

Alice Weston (10)
The Minster CE Primary School, Warminster

Night-Time Friend

I lie waiting for her to emerge out of the darkness.
She says, 'No matter what happens, I will always be there for you.'
She's dressed in a gleaming white dress, her hair as black as ebony.
As she walks, there are flowers in her footsteps.
She lives in my wardrobe with pictures of me sleeping in my
>   cosy bed.

Asiya Kaplankiran (10)
The Minster CE Primary School, Warminster

My Mum

Sometimes my mum is cross and goes red-hot,
Sometimes my mum is very nice and sometimes she's not.
She does my cooking, cleaning, washing and tidies my room
And very often you will see her with her broom.

Mum has to work so hard to look after us,
But she doesn't mind, she knows it's a must.
She cares for us when we are ill
And sometimes we go for a walk up Cley Hill.

I love my mum, I'm sure you can see
And so do the rest of my family.
She gives us cuddles when we are sad,
But sometimes we are naughty and that makes her mad.

My mum is so kind,
She never seems to mind
And when it's sunny,
She gives us pocket money.

My mum has a heart full of love
And she's always there for us.
My mum will always be my mum,
As we all only have one.

Jack Cray (7)
The Minster CE Primary School, Warminster

Stranger

I see your shadow in the valley.
I hear your sinister scratches in the night-time moon.
Dogs bark as you're sitting below the misty sky.
Stranger,
Why not show your face?
I can't get your screech out of my head.
Stranger, just tell me a word,
Make a sound so I know you are there.

Charlotte Mole (10)
The Minster CE Primary School, Warminster

Kennings What Am I?

Flapping flipper
Swift swimmer
Fin pointer
High jumper
Sliding dasher
Slippery skin
Vivid surfer
Clicking clappers.

A: dolphin

Louise Bodman (10)
The Minster CE Primary School, Warminster

Kennings What Am I?

Corner croucher
Net maker
Patient predator
Meal watcher
Lunch catcher
Foe eater
Silent sleeper
Short liver.

A: spider.

Alex Smith (11)
The Minster CE Primary School, Warminster

Kennings What Am I?

Meat eater
Evil killer
Cub lover
Meat chewer
Fiery fur
Spotty wonder
Sneaking down
Crouching ready.

A: cheetah.

Benjamin Rudin (10)
The Minster CE Primary School, Warminster

Kennings What Am I?

Hairy bodied
Long tailed
Banana muncher
Bug cruncher
Monkey inspector
Tree swinger
Coloured face
Red bottomed.

A: baboon.

Giuseppe G & Sam Couch (11)
The Minster CE Primary School, Warminster

Kennings What Am I?

Brain washer
Wing runner
Ballet dancer
Card getter
Foul faller
Goal hanger
Ball chaser
Skilful player.

A: football player.

Emma Ledbury (11)
The Minster CE Primary School, Warminster

Kennings What Am I?

Spying eyes
Feathery ball
Air swooper
Sky diver
Hovering predator
Prey killer
Day sleeper
Night hunter.

A: owl.

Bobby Darvill (10)
The Minster CE Primary School, Warminster

Kennings What Am I?

Trouble maker
High sleeper
Vine grabber
Branch hanger
Long armer
Branch swinger
Hairy scary
Cheeky freaky.

A: monkey.

Thomas Reynolds (11)
The Minster CE Primary School, Warminster

Kennings What Am I?

Cheeky creature
Fast mover
Very hairy
Bottom scary
Fast nicker
Baby crier
Banana muncher
Tiny finder.

A: monkey.

Lauren Payne (10)
The Minster CE Primary School, Warminster

Once Upon A Time

Once upon a time,
There were wizards and kings,
Mermaids and unicorns,
Pegasus, who had powerful wings.

Elves to make mischief
And dragons to slay,
Giants to kill,
Debts of honour to pay.

Many mythical creatures,
Many months, June and May,
Wise old centaurs,
To help you find your way.

Queens to sacrifice,
Witches to conquer,
Princes to rescue,
Princesses.
All this was possible,
Once upon a time.

Ashleigh Moore (10)
Trowbridge Parochial CE Junior School, Trowbridge

Blue Secrets

Mountains as thick as thieves
Guarding treasure as smooth as blue velvet
Waiting for the sun to come their way.

Beneath the dappled mountains
That stand as proud as preening peacocks
The water hides a precious secret
Never to be revealed.

Rhoda Martin (10)
Walton Primary School, Walton

Dreams

I dream of woodland glades,
With ponies and unicorns
Under the shade.
I dream of mermaids
Splashing in the sea,
Giggling with happiness and glee.
I see the waves splish, splash, roar,
Washing up shells on the sandy floor.
I dream of dragons,
In a rocky cave,
Breathing out fire,
Sparks and flames.
I dream of wizards and witches,
Casting spells,
Butterflies fluttering,
All by themselves.
I dream of my own house,
Full of books,
So I peek inside and take a look
And that just goes to show
How my imagination grows.

Zoe Cotton (10)
Walton Primary School, Walton

Snake

Here is a snake
Proud and strong
When he is in his cage
He looks very long.
He is white and black
Smooth scales on his back
He is chunky and thick
And I named him Cedrick.

Carys Taylor (11)
Walton Primary School, Walton

Apple Cider

Here I am, in the trees,
Resting in the sunlight.
Now here comes a swarm of bees,
Yellow bodies bright.

There are sheep below me,
Looking up with black eyes.
They stare at me hungrily,
They are very greedy guys.

Suddenly I am found,
Hiding up there in the tree.
I am taken to the ground,
And there's a face looking at me.

I am carried to a barn,
For some reason I don't know.
Then suddenly, in alarm,
I am crushed with one blow.

I now know why it was,
I was taken and made wider.
It was, as you can see,
To be made into cider.

Victoria Lloyd (10)
Walton Primary School, Walton

The End (Of The Holiday)

Walking along the beach,
Sand crushing between my toes,
Tide water trickling onto my feet,
Seagulls swooping overhead,
On their way home,
Just like me.

Eadie Bartlett-Mates (10)
Walton Primary School, Walton

My Pony

I have a pony called Sam
And sometimes I give him some ham.
He likes to eat grass all day
And it doesn't cost very much for his hay.

In the winter he goes in the stable,
Although it is very run down.
My pony lives in a village,
Not in a noisy town.

I love my pony very much,
But his breed is not Dutch.
I hope he lives as long as my old pony,
But I hope he doesn't get very bony!

Sophie Linham (9)
Walton Primary School, Walton

What A Rhyme

Little Jack Horner sat on a rock
He saw Humpty Dumpty and fainted in shock.

Humpty Dumpty bounced over to Jack
And gave him a great big pat on the back.

Little Bo Peep came with her sheep
Just as Little Jack Horner took a great leap
And landed on Little Bo Peep.

This is the end of Little Jack Horner
Who spent his life in his corner
This is the end of Little Bo Peep
Who can no longer look after her sheep.

Katie Devenish (11)
Walton Primary School, Walton

Guess Who?

A little face, with little ears,
Lives in a cage with sawdust,
He is so cute, he is so tiny,
You're right, he's my hamster.

Long, white whiskers,
Black and white fur,
Likes to catch mice,
I want him forever and ever,
You're right, he's my cat.

Likes company, likes hugs,
Likes playing Frisbee,
I love him so much,
Good sense of smell,
He plays ball so well,
You're right, he's my dog.

Likes chilling out, likes playing,
Likes animals and friends,
Likes singing, doing grade three,
Loves her family,
You're right, it's me!

Gabrielle Govier (10)
Walton Primary School, Walton

Summer Sky

Palm trees like enormous
Feather dusters
Dust the blue sky
Skyscrapers wait like rockets
Ready for take-off
Roads snake here and there
Leading who knows where!

Melissa Davies (10)
Walton Primary School, Walton

Night-Time

Wind is howling
Cats are prowling
People sleep
Floorboards creak.

People wake
Hear the quake
Buildings rumble
Small things tumble.

Scary eyes
Big surprise
Made you jump
What's that thump?

People groan
Others moan
Lots of blood
What a thug.

Blue lights
Exciting nights
Big crowds
Why so loud?

Be quiet
It's a riot
Such commotion
And emotion.

Jack Clarke (10)
Walton Primary School, Walton

The Sea And Me

The dolphins dive from the sea
Scattering sparkling crystals on me
They dive back under to their sea home
Where they have an undersea dome.
A colourful world not yet discovered
Which I have uncovered
Full of pretty coral
And my best friend, Oral
Who lives in an undersea world.

Amelia Wall (9)
Walton Primary School, Walton

Chairs

Comfortable chairs, smooth and
Squidgy.
Hard chairs, lumpy and
Bumpy.
Armchairs with castors.
Inflatable chairs, bright colours.
Rocking chairs, comfortable
Cushions.

Chelsie Pryer (10)
Webber's CE Primary School, Wellington

Chairs

When I sit in a pew . . . I wriggle.
When I slouch in an armchair . . . I feel squashed.
When I perch in a wheelchair . . . I'm uncomfortable.
When I bounce on my springy chair . . . I start to bubble.
But when I sink into my sofa I can't be more relaxed.

Elizabeth Firth (10)
Webber's CE Primary School, Wellington

Wheelchair

I have an electric wheelchair and it's new.
It's like a throne or dentist's chair to me.
I just relax and gently tilt the joystick, oh!

I have an electric wheelchair and it's new.
As I never get exhausted, sink or flop,
At home I sit in a comfy rocking chair,
Very cushioned too, hey . . .

I have an electric wheelchair and it's new.
I am disabled for my lifetime.
That is why I have an electric wheelchair.
I have an electric wheelchair and it's new.

Fred Cooper (10)
Webber's CE Primary School, Wellington

Office Chair

I sit in the office chair,
I sit at the computer in the office chair,
I sit at the table in the office chair,
I sit and watch TV in the office chair,
I sit and wheel the office chair around the kitchen floor,
I deliberately squeak the office chair on the kitchen floor.

Georgina Dornom (10)
Webber's CE Primary School, Wellington

Slicing Scissors

The sound of snapping scissors slicing into its enemy.
Chopping and destroying it into tiny pieces.
The paper is now in pieces of annihilation.

Oliver Baker-Whyte (11)
Webber's CE Primary School, Wellington

The Killing Chair

He was led up to the chair.
The dreaded electric chair.

He was buckled in the chair.
The dreaded electric chair.

He was killed by the chair.
The dreaded electric chair.

He sat limp in the chair.
The dreaded electric chair.

Toby Bonvoisin (10)
Webber's CE Primary School, Wellington

Scissors

S cissors are amazing things,
C utting through paper and lots of things,
I use scissors for lots of uses,
S licing, chopping through the cardboard,
S nipping fast, through the hedge,
O bserve the swiftly moving scissors,
R ound the corners of the paper,
S cissors are amazing things.

Jess Leyland (11)
Webber's CE Primary School, Wellington

South American Shoes

I can see some new shoes in the window.
I wish I had some.
Everyone in the street has shoes.
Except me.
Cold feet.
I wish I had warm feet.

Pete Thorburn (11)
Webber's CE Primary School, Wellington

Colours

Colours of death and colours of life.
Colours of day and colours of night.
Colours of gloom and colours of scope.
Colours of joy and colours of hope.
Colours of age and colours of youth.
Colours of lies and colours of truth.
Colours of tears and colours of smiles.
Colours of burdens and colours of trials.
Colours of day and colours of night.
Colours of death and colours of life.

Stephanie Howe (11)
Webber's CE Primary School, Wellington

Scissors Cinquain

Snipping
Splitting, slitting
Parchment split, words are halved
Shearing sheep, snipping hairs, wool gone
Scissors.

Emma Selby (10)
Webber's CE Primary School, Wellington

Pencil Cinquain

Pencil
Have a pencil
Especially for you
Printed with your name on its wood
Pencil.

Laura White (10)
Webber's CE Primary School, Wellington

My New Scissors

I've got some new scissors today,
They're as sharp as razor blades.
The handles are blue,
Really shiny.

I love my new scissors,
I can cut with one *snip.*
My brother really likes them,
But I am the only person who can use them
And the best thing about them is
They're brand *new.*

Lucy Stansfield (11)
Webber's CE Primary School, Wellington

Trimming Lessons

Snappy, squeaky, scraping,
That's my pair of scissors.
Trimming people's hair so neat,
I am the best hairdresser.
Slicing, slipping, every now and then,
That's it, work over, time to go home for tea,
But before that, I cut my pet sheep, Kee.
I clip, I cut, the blunt blades squeaky,
Chopping, swishing, swooshing,
Giving a trim for dear old Kee.

Sam Barker (11)
Webber's CE Primary School, Wellington

In My Dream I Saw . . .

In my dream I saw
A silent spider spinning swiftly
Before the sun rose and hurrying
Before the morning dew
Crept over the still land.

In my dream I heard
The chatter of cockatoos
Readying themselves for
Their flights through the swirling mists
To the fruitful trees
In the pale, orange glow
Of the watery, round sun.

In my dream I saw
A golden jaguar leap the silvery waterhole
In the wilderness
As seamlessly as a salmon
Gallantly fighting the mighty falls.

In my dream I saw
The shiny scales of a greenish-blue gecko
Shaped like diamonds, as sharp as spears
Glinting in the noontide sun
As it snoozed on a mossy log.

In my dream I heard
The moon gently
Lulling, hushing the darkening land
Falling softly to slumber.

In my dream I saw
The chorus of the jungle
Shaking the sleepy sun
Out of its humble home to roam the
Great blue skies once more.

Lydia Bartlett (11)
Wells Cathedral Junior School, Wells

In My Dream I Saw . . .

In my dream I saw
A dirty dragon dining
On a donkey
In the safety of his den.

In my dream I heard
The puzzling song of a sphinx
Singing about the world
And all its creatures.

In my dream I saw
A silver lion
With golden wings
Fly like an angel.

In my dream I saw
A dragon scale
Glisten like a diamond.

In my dream I heard
The wind
Running through the mountains.

In my dream I saw
A unicorn
As fast as an arrow from a bow
Shooting through the sparkling snow.

Caspar Green (11)
Wells Cathedral Junior School, Wells

In My Dream I Saw . . .

In my dream I saw a silent snail slithering snakily
Across a grassy field.

In my dream I heard
A dog's tail thumping
On a welcome mat.

In my dream I saw
A wonderful gleaming silver sloth
As bright as the stars.

In my dream I saw
A dolphin's beak
As round as a pineapple.

In my dream I heard
The sun arguing with the wind
Saying, 'Go away you horrible burst of cold air.'

In my dream I saw
A fluffy-headed chick
Shouting to its friends
While eating a wriggly worm.

Nellie Barnes (10)
Wells Cathedral Junior School, Wells

In My Dream I Saw . . .

In my dream I saw
A perfect penguin play politely
On the Antarctic plain.

In my dream I heard,
The buzz of busy bees
And the skipping of a horse.

In my dream I saw
A silver unicorn prance,
As proudly as a peacock.

In my dream I saw
A swaying tail of a fantail fish,
Shaped like a triangle.

In my dream I heard
The winter bust
Through the wall of summer.

In my dream I saw
A rabbit hop so fast, it was a
Lightning bolt, bringing brightness.

Lucy Austin (10)
Wells Cathedral Junior School, Wells

In My Dream I Saw . . .

In my dream I saw
A lovely leopard languidly leaping
Through the jungle's plants.

In my dream I heard
The screech of a monkey
Swinging from tree to tree.

In my dream I saw
An electric-blue angel fish
Glide through the water
As elegantly as an ice skater.

In my dream I saw
The bright red sun setting
Shaped like circles from
A tropical butterfly's wing.

In my dream I heard
The summer breeze whispering
To the moon as it rose in the
Evening sky.

In my dream I saw
The silvery-white moon smiling down on me
With pools of moonbeams washing over me
Like the sea washing over turtles when returning to the sea.

Caroline Taylor (11)
Wells Cathedral Junior School, Wells

In My Dream I Saw . . .

In my dream I saw
A sower scattering seeds swiftly
Along the dry plains.

In my dream I heard
The howl of a lonely husky
Lost in the wilderness
And the singing of the zo-sing bird
Humming a song not yet known.

In my dream I saw
A purple lizard looking
As light as a feather
Yet his story's unknown.

In my dream I saw
The large eagle's claw
Shaped like a holly leaf.

In my dream I heard
The wind in a racing car
Speeding all the way.

In my dream I saw
A man as an iceberg
A telephone answering itself
Six sloths snoozing
But all of these things remain locked up in my mind
Not quite real.

Nicola Kingston (10)
Wells Cathedral Junior School, Wells

In My Dream I Saw . . .

In my dream I saw
A blue buoy bounce blindly
By the shore.

In my dream I heard
The crack of it splitting
And the cry of the victorious sea.

In my dream I saw
A silver seal dance
As swift as a swallow.

In my dream I saw
The lone sea puss' tentacle
Stretching like a cat.

In my dream I saw
The silent nothingness
Being still.

In my dream I saw
The rippling sunlight smile and beckon
Bringing me up to the summer sun
I gasp for air
And on me the world will stare.

Alex Moore (11)
Wells Cathedral Junior School, Wells

In My Dream I Saw . . .

In my dream I saw
A brown duck dangerously dive
In a shallow pool of custard.

In my dream I heard
A pleasant purr of a Persian cat
In the dark, black night.

In my dream I saw
The cold eyes of the Devil
Glinting like cats' eyes.

In my dream I saw
A purple head shaped
Like a banana.

In my dream I heard
The moon yawning heavily
As its time was up.

In my dream I saw
The moon slowly drop
Into the valley sunshine
'Shine over the little dames
It said as the sun came.

Emma Murton (11)
Wells Cathedral Junior School, Wells

In My Dream I Saw . . .

In my dream I saw
A small sylph sucking sherbet
Behind the long church wall.

In my dream I heard
The crash of lightning
And the crying of a baby.

In my dream I saw
A purple dinosaur
As small as an ant.

In my dream I saw
The decapitated head of a pelican
Shaped like a frog.

In my dream I heard
The crescent moon
Mow the lawn.

In my dream I saw
A giant with a ginormous head
A star switching off the light
A breeze blowing swiftly
And the sun going to bed
To rest its weary head.

Charles Brice (10)
Wells Cathedral Junior School, Wells

In My Dream I Saw . . .

In my dream I saw
A pretty pony prancing privately
Practising moves for a party.

In my dream I saw
The beat of a pop party
Starting at the end of a long day.

In my dream I saw
A lilac dog running across a field
As fast as a leopard.

In my dream I saw
The tail of a dog waggling happily
Like a streak of wind.

In my dream I heard
The wind whistle
As it came right by my window.

In my dream I saw
A dog talk to itself
Howling in the wind.

Clara Armstrong (10)
Wells Cathedral Junior School, Wells

In My Dream I Saw . . .

In my dream I saw
A perfect penguin prance
Across the white-hot desert.

In my dream I heard
The whoosh of a swift
Flying through the perfect blue ocean
Round Hawaii.

In my dream I saw
A golden phoenix
Hot as a star
In the beautiful black sky.

In my dream I saw
A colourful rainbow
Like the beak of a toucan
Resting on a mango tree.

In my dream I heard
The moon snoring
Over all the Earth
Lying in perfect silence
In the darkness.

In my dream I saw
A solid silver moon
Swim across the sky
Shooting dim rays to my eyes
Telling me to stay asleep
And lie in my thoughts
Till morning.

James Browning (11)
Wells Cathedral Junior School, Wells

In My Dream I Saw . . .

In my dream I saw
A crazy cow croaking continuously
Down the ditch.

In my dream I heard
The miaow of a cat
Washing herself
She is a fluffy ball.

In my dream I saw
A desert
Hot as the sun
Burning bright sun.

In my dream I saw
The white moon
Like a circle of peace caught in the sky.

In my dream I heard
Spring bursting with fruits
Struggle out of their buds
Talking to the others
In the beaming sunlight.

In my dream I saw
The white-faced moon
Pushing out of the earth
Turning off all the lights of the day
Making everyone everywhere feel like falling asleep
As quietly as mice
In the night.

Sam Tincknell (10)
Wells Cathedral Junior School, Wells

In My Dream I Saw . . .

In my dream I saw
A darling damsel in distress
Dancing daintily
In the highest room
In the tallest tower.

In my dream I heard
The thump of a rabbit's hind leg
Warning his children
That the wolf was coming.

In my dream I saw
A blue dog
As wet as the sea
In the early sunset.

In my dream I saw
The bushy sun
Like a kitten's tail
Sweeping the floor.

In my dream I heard
The fierce frost
Winning the race against the sun
Cheering with the hail.

In my dream I saw
The ill, pale-faced moon in bed
With the stars looking after him
The sound sun shining across the world
Waiting for the winter wind to be hurled.

Abigail Walsh (10)
Wells Cathedral Junior School, Wells

In My Dream I Saw . . .

In my dream I saw
A hungry hyena hunting
Across the African plain.

In my dream I heard
A howl of a wolf
Running by
In the dark blue
Of the ocean.

In my dream I saw
The beaming sun
Red as fire
Silently beaming down.

In my dream I saw
The stars glistening
Like street lamps
In the ruby-red sky.

In my dream I heard
The winter wind
Whistling to the
Dead, fallen leaves.

In my dream I saw
The silver-faced moon
Sleeping in the midnight sky
Stars silently sparkling
Like diamonds in the sky.

Anna Durbacz (11)
Wells Cathedral Junior School, Wells

In My Dream I Saw . . .

In my dream I saw a pretty puffin
Prance on a rock
In the middle of the Pipi sea

In my dream I heard the moan of a whale
And the creak of a hearty pirate shipwreck
Sinking in the sand
With the spirit of the black-hearted crew

In my dream I saw a lilac Lia
Pick berries off a tree
Like a nomad finding an oasis

In my dream I saw the flick of a thick vixen's tail
Shaped as a worn, golden feather duster
That Cinderella used

In my dream I heard
Spring peep
Through the blanket of winter snow
And sprinkle the world with daffodils

In my dream I saw
The giant of our world
Spin slowly into the black, deep hole of our universe
Making my head blank
Warning me to wake up
For a new day has begun.

Eleanor Seaton (11)
Wells Cathedral Junior School, Wells

In My Dream I Saw . . .

In my dream I saw
Seven white whales waltzing with walruses
At a ball.

In my dream I heard
The silent swish of the deep blue sea
And the splashing of waves.

In my dream I saw
The bright green eyes of a sabre-toothed tiger
Darting like a dragonfly.

In my dream I saw
A slowly moving panther's paw
Shaped like a daisy.

In my dream I heard
Spring waking up
To an early morning swim.

In my dream I saw
The silver-faced moon
Mutter to itself about
How bossy the sun was
Being that morning.
As the extremely, exhausted elephant awoke
Yawning, yawning, yawning.

Polly Baker (11)
Wells Cathedral Junior School, Wells

In My Dream I Saw . . .

In my dream I saw,
A cunning cat creep carefully,
Behind the kitchen door.

In my dream I heard,
The fluttering of a mother's wings,
And the chirping of her hungry babies.

In my dream I saw,
A blue dog climb a tree,
As swiftly as a cat.

In my dream I saw,
The beautiful tiger's tail,
Swing, as briskly as the wind.

In my dream I heard,
The spring,
Leap into action,
As the flowers started to grow.

In my dream I saw,
The hot-faced sun,
Walk around the sky,
So silently, so soundly, saying,
'Hello day, night goodbye!'

Emily Phillips (10)
Wells Cathedral Junior School, Wells

In My Dream I Saw . . .

In my dream I saw
A fast, furious figure
Running round the room.

In my dream I heard
The birds in the trees
Singing and tweeting in the sun's beam.

In my dream I saw
A bright green fox dancing gracefully
Like a balanced ballerina.

In my dream I saw
The fine fox's tail
Delicately swaying to and fro
Like a whip slashing up and down.

In my dream I saw
The wind bursting in
Whispering softly through the air.

In my dream I saw
A giant with a toothbrush
He was screaming *ow!*
Whilst tugging a big black dog
And then I woke up and said, *'How?'*

Henry Bruegger (11)
Wells Cathedral Junior School, Wells

In My Dream I Saw . . .

In my dream I saw
A clever cat carefully climb
Up a tall, narrow tree.

In my dream I heard
The hypnotic tick of a clock
Working at a pace so slow and simple.

In my dream I saw
A red-hot sun
As hot as fire
Giving great heat.

In my dream I saw
The bright stars
Like shining silver pearls
Trapped in the moonlight.

In my dream I heard
The wild wind whistling to itself
Shrieking at the rustling leaves.

In my dream I saw
The white-faced moon
Sliding across the dark sky
Casting lengths of shadow
Pulling my bright body
Across the bed
Like a poisonous snake
Lifting its head.

Ralph Morton (10)
Wells Cathedral Junior School, Wells

In My Dream I Saw . . .

In my dream I saw
A hiccupping hippopotamus
Hopping heavily
Across the smelly swamp.

In my dream I heard
The song of the birds
Sing out to each other
While in the green grass and the trees.

In my dream I saw
A silvery-white unicorn
Leaping as wildly as a bear.

In my dream I saw
The sharp teeth of a shark
Caught in the beam of the sun.

In my dream I heard
The solemn sun
Calling for day.

In my dream I saw
A silver-faced moon
Crawling for the day
Over the high mountains
Throwing the net of darkness
Pulling my golden cat out of his tree
Like a yellow rose.

Georgia Crumlish (11)
Wells Cathedral Junior School, Wells

In My Dream I Saw . . .

In my dream I saw
A mischievous monkey move mysteriously
Through the tangling trees.

In my dream I heard
The rustle of a ladybug twitching
And the flickering of the last flame of a candle.

In my dream I saw
A ghostly-white unicorn stampede
As swiftly as a cheetah.

In my dream I saw
The deformed, penetrating eyes of an ancient mummy
Shaped like pancakes.

In my dream I heard
The wind huskily
Whistle tunelessly in the breeze.

In my dream I saw
The citrus-yellow feathers of a
Hallabungah bird flutter gracefully
Hypnotizing those miles below into a solid slumber
Making all those feel as cool as cucumber.

Miranda Lim (11)
Wells Cathedral Junior School, Wells

In My Dream I Saw . . .

In my dream I saw
A lurking lion lying lazily
In the dry grass.

In my dream I heard
The snapping of an alligator
And the miaow of a cat.

In my dream I saw
The tall giraffe's neck
Moving like a snake on the run.

In my dream I saw
An aqua goldfish race across the ocean
Like a shooting star.

In my dream I heard
The autumn push past me.

In my dream I saw
The white-faced moon
Drifting behind the hills
And sending the sleepy sun
To wake everyone.

Charlotte Storer (11)
Wells Cathedral Junior School, Wells

In My Dream

In my dream I saw
A pretty, pink, prancing pony,
Pounding its hooves on the uneven sand.

In my dream I heard
The thump of elephants' feet
And the ripping of trees
Coming down at the forest edge.

In my dream I saw
A perfect purple dolphin,
As shiny as a piece of gold.

In my dream I saw
A sleek cat's tail,
Shaped like a long banana.

In my dream I heard
The wind whispering with the trees,
Playing with the fallen leaves.

In my dream I saw
The cold-faced moon,
Staring (rudely) at the stars,
Showing shadowy light in the dark night.

Elizabeth Burke (11)
Wells Cathedral Junior School, Wells

In My Dream I Saw . . .

In my dream I saw
A pretty pony pouncing
Across the fields.

In my dream I heard
The distant bleat of a sheep
Running over the moors
And in the misty sea a shark
As black as night baring his jaws.

In my dream I saw
The yellow sun hot as an oven
That gives gold lawns.

In my dream I saw
The bright moon
Like a doleful dolphin's eye
Caught in the sky.

In my dream I heard
The whistling whinnies
Of unicorns talking to the endless woods.

In my dream I saw
The golden-headed sun
Storming up in the distance
Casting ropes of light
Tugging me out of my sheets
Like hypnotized owls from the skies.

Jess Pullen (11)
Wells Cathedral Junior School, Wells

In My Dream I Saw . . .

In my dream I saw
A pink pelican politely pecking
Across the riverbank.

In my dream I saw
A whooshing crew of birds
Swoop across the calm, blue sky.

In my dream I saw
The gleaming sun
Boiling like lava
Reflecting on the tearing ocean.

In my dream I saw
The glowing moon
Like slimy snail trails
Appear in the black, starry sky.

In my dream I heard
The wind whistle
Howling down my ear
Whispering to the swifting trees.

In my dream I saw
The silver-faced moon
Pulling through the clouds
Casting ropes of yellow rays
Blacking me but
Without a shout.

Sebastian Hoyle (11)
Wells Cathedral Junior School, Wells

My Dream

In my dream I saw
A bouncy bunny
Bounce across the fields of blue.

In my dream I heard
A caterpillar crunch
Under a large foot creeping.

In my dream I saw
A red centipede
As quick as the winds of change.

In my dream I saw
A frog's leg
Shaped like a pool of water.

In my dream I heard
Spring calling out to me
'Drink my pure, sweet drink.'

In my dream I saw
The sparkling stars
Jump over the sun
Into the deep blue sky
Swaying to and fro
Getting me to sleep saying
'Secrets, I'm sure to keep.'

Marianne Bruce (10)
Wells Cathedral Junior School, Wells

In My Dream I Saw . . .

In my dream I saw
A humble hamster hopscotch horridly
Across the schoolyard.

In my dream I heard
The cruel laughs of teenagers
Destroying themselves
In the dusty, boarded-up houses
In the street.

In my dream I saw
The turquoise frog
Croaking like a sore throat.

In my dream I saw
The young horse's feet
Shaped like an egg.

In my dream I heard
The mellow sun cursing
The winter wind.

In my dream I saw
The ghost-like moon
Glare at the sun
Spitefully skidding
Across the sky, joking around
Like he was kidding.

Jess McGee (10)
Wells Cathedral Junior School, Wells

In My Dream I Saw . . .

In my dream I saw,
A sleek swan swim swiftly
Over the smooth pond.

In my dream I heard,
The tiny quack of yellow ducklings,
Daring to swim
In the clear, crystal lakes.

In my dream I saw,
A pearly-white unicorn,
As beautiful as a star,
Pawing the silver ground.

In my dream I saw,
The fiery sun,
Like a trustful tiger's eyes.

In my dream I heard,
The great, white moon,
Whispering to the many constellations
In the dark blue sky.

In my dream I saw,
The golden clouds
Play tag
Over the bright blue pool,
Like young children playing with me.

In my dream I heard,
The soft, sweet chirps
Of birds,
Singing a serenade
Of peace.

Victoria Toulson-Clarke (11)
Wells Cathedral Junior School, Wells

In My Dream I Saw . . .

In my dream I saw
A crafty caterpillar crawl carefully
Around a leaf

In my dream I heard
The deafening drawl of dragons
Doing somersaults
In the bright green body of the grass

In my dream I saw
A yellow snake
As blinding as the sun

In my dream I saw
The pale moon
Like a cold rabbit's tail
In a blue net

In my dream I heard
The summer sun
Singing to itself
Whispering with the trees

In my dream I saw
The white moon
Crawl over the fields
Throwing white beams
Pushing my sleeping self up from bed
Like a bird about to be fed.

Cervinia Wakelin-Gilden (11)
Wells Cathedral Junior School, Wells

In My Dream I Saw . . .

In my dream I saw
A puffy parrot proudly peek
On a wooden fence.

In my dream I heard
The yakky yelling of hyenas
Tickling themselves
In the bleak outback desert plain of the East.

In my dream I heard
A pink platypus
Eating like a pig.

In my dream I saw
A tongue of a dog
Licking like the wind.

In my dream I heard
The bitter wind
Whistle to itself.

In my dream I saw
The blue-faced moon smile
Casting beams of joy
Tugging my lifeless self
Up from death
Like deer springing up
From the plain.

Alexander Goodliff (10)
Wells Cathedral Junior School, Wells

In My Dream I Saw . . .

In my dream I saw
A perfect puffin playing peacefully
On a dainty, gold rock
In the deep red sea.

In my dream I heard
The quiet wish-wash of the waves
Climbing up the white sanded beach
Under a beautiful summer sunset.

In my dream I saw
A piebald panda devouring leaves
As daintily as a duchess.

In my dream I saw
A blue and red parakeet's wing
Shaped like a shining crescent moon.

In my dream I heard
The sun drying the washing,
Jabbering to the shirts, like a chattering monkey.

In my dream I saw
The pale-faced moon
Battle with the wild winter wind.

Alice Laing (10)
Wells Cathedral Junior School, Wells

In My Dream I Saw . . .

In my dream I saw
An enormous elephant emerge eastward
And storm through the west.

In my dream I heard
The sound of a bird chirp
And the snoring of a lioness.

In my dream I saw
A pink crocodile emerge
As swift as a cheetah.

In my dream I saw
The slithery snake's tongue
Shaped like a sniggering hyena.

In my dream I heard
Autumn gently
Coughing.

In my dream I saw
A rabbit who was the wind
Singing softly.

Timothy Coppen (10)
Wells Cathedral Junior School, Wells

In My Dream I Saw . . .

In my dream I saw
A wriggly worm wriggle weirdly
Down into the mud.

In my dream I heard
The roar of a lion and the running of zebras
On the African plains.

In my dream I saw
A blue and luminous green dragon breathing purple flames
As angrily as a wolf without her cubs.

In my dream I saw
The shiny green eyes of a lizard
Glowing in the night sky.

In my dream I heard
The moon whispering to the early morning sun
As it skated past him like a bird gliding through the air.

In my dream I saw
The blood-red neck of a tulip
Muttering to itself and dancing down on Dover's dark earth.

James Brand (11)
Wells Cathedral Junior School, Wells

In My Dream I Saw . . .

In my dream I saw
A delicate dove dive deeply
Into the water.

In my dream I heard
The choo-chooing calling train
Coming home from Canterbury.

In my dream I saw
A bright pink elephant eating
As quickly as a pig.

In my dream I saw
A squishy nose
Shaped like a heart.

In my dream I heard
The spring springing while
Chattering cheerfully.

In my dream I saw
The silver-faced moon
Smiling smartly singing songs.

Ella Kelly (11)
Wells Cathedral Junior School, Wells

In My Dream I Saw . . .

In my dream I saw
A poofy pigeon plodding
Across the grass.

In my dream I heard
The sniffle snuffles of a horse
Galloping into the night sky.

In my dream I saw
A lime fish swimming
Like a calm wave.

In my dream I saw
The whitest part of the snow fox's paw.

In my dream I heard
The moon lighting up
To talk to the sky.

In my dream I saw
The white-faced unicorn
Struggling over the hills
And the hairy hares followed.

Samantha Peirce (10)
Wells Cathedral Junior School, Wells

In My Dream I Saw . . .

In my dream I saw
A lively leopard leaping lazily
On a hot afternoon.

In my dream I saw
A gathering of people
Partying.

In my dream I saw
A purple otter eating
As loudly as an elephant fighting.

In my dream I saw
An annoying fly's leg
Shaped like a circle.

In my dream I heard
The wind shouting.

In my dream I saw
The wind whistling water
Whistling up a tidal wave.

Georgia Geipel (10)
Wells Cathedral Junior School, Wells

In My Dream I Saw . . .

In my dream I saw
An enormous elephant eagerly edge
Across the high cliff.

In my dream I heard
The roar of a vicious lion
And the screeching of his cubs.

In my dream I saw
A lilac slug squeak
As quiet as a mouse.

In my dream I heard
The stars whistle to me
Like the owner of a dog.

In my dream I saw
The blue-finned fish
Leap out of the water
I saw a bird wash itself in my bath
Using my super scrubbing brush.

Jessica Orrett (10)
Wells Cathedral Junior School, Wells

In My Dream I Saw . . .

In my dream I saw
A leprechaun leap lightly.

In my dream I heard
A scratching, screeching squirrel.

In my dream I saw
A black sky let out a cold wind.

In my dream I saw
Fluffy, furry fur.

In my dream I saw
A moon merge mistily.

Alexander Hopperton (10)
Wells Cathedral Junior School, Wells

In My Dream I Saw . . .

In my dream I saw
A dreary day dawning
Ushering away the dark night.

In my dream I heard
The chirruping of a newborn chickadee
And the shrieking of a dying sun.

In my dream I saw
The crooked beak of the ravenous eagle
Shaped like a sharp, glinting fishing hook.

In my dream I heard
The summer sun slam the black door
To hatred and darkness.

In my dream I saw
The bloodthirsty figure of war
Tear down the shining veil of peace
And the suffering stars screaming
For lost lives and strife to cease.

Sorcha Kennedy (10)
Wells Cathedral Junior School, Wells

Kerry

You are the water flowing down the stream.
You are the goal I kick in football.
You are the fizz in my Coke.
You are the tide rushing up on the pebbles.
You are the pink rose in my garden.
You are the rushing wind.
You are the ray of sunshine in my hair.
You are the god of the growing flowers.
You are the sugar on my apple pie.
I have never had a better friend than you.

Jade Redfern (9)
West Chinnock CE Primary School, Crewkerne

I Used To Be

I used to be young, but now I am old.
I used to have blonde hair, but now I have grey hair.
I used to have teeth, but now I have none.
I used to have a smooth face, but now it is wrinkly.
I used to be ten, but now I am ninety-seven.

Kerry Roberts (10)
West Chinnock CE Primary School, Crewkerne

Batty About Bats

The bat is a wonderful creature
Whose sonar can feel every feature
But they're not bad
There's no blood to be had
Not even that of your teacher!

Becky Doherty (11)
West Chinnock CE Primary School, Crewkerne

My Gerbil - Haiku

My gerbil runs fast
Like the wind up in the trees
And digs like a mole.

Joe Leighton (11)
West Chinnock CE Primary School, Crewkerne

On the Farm - Haiku

I work every day
Putting muck over the fields
To make the crops grow.

Jack Hawker (11)
West Chinnock CE Primary School, Crewkerne

Mum

You're the blue sky of a spring day
You're the sound of a robin singing on a bit of holly
You're the sparkling dew on the first day of autumn
You're the stars over me at night
You're the raindrops on the spiderweb
You're my mum.

Sarah-Jane Nicholson (11)
West Chinnock CE Primary School, Crewkerne

Happiness

Happiness is the colour bright yellow
It tastes like ripe oranges
It smells like ripe strawberries
It looks like a sunflower
It sounds like a dandelion waving in the wind
It feels like rabbit skin.

Denis Cozens (7)
West Coker CE VC Primary School, Yeovil

Love

Love is a pinky-red colour.
Love tastes like strawberries covered with cream
And smells like a bright red rose.
Love looks like a naked woman
And sounds like wedding bells.
Love feels like a furry red heart.

Christopher Townsend (10)
West Coker CE VC Primary School, Yeovil

Love

Love is bright red
And tastes like chocolate fudge
It smells like a roast dinner
Love looks like a bright blue dolphin
And sounds like the breeze rustling the trees
Love feels like a soft, fluffy rabbit.

Sarah Fudge (9)
West Coker CE VC Primary School, Yeovil

Love

Love is the colour of red roses
It tastes like chocolate ice cream
It smells like bubbling gravy
It looks like a bird flying in the sky
Love sounds like a happy dog
Love feels like a furry cat.

Dale Antcliffe (9)
West Coker CE VC Primary School, Yeovil

Excitement

Excitement is the colour of a strawberry milkshake,
It tastes like chocolate
And smells like a beautiful red rose.
It sounds like a pig snorting.
Excitement is when it is nearly your birthday.

Jade Whittle (10)
West Coker CE VC Primary School, Yeovil

Hate

Hate is black
It tastes like rotten apples
Hate smells like a dead badger
It looks like a dark shadow
Hate sounds like thunder
It feels like an adult hedgehog's back.

Sophie Hackett (9)
West Coker CE VC Primary School, Yeovil

Sad

Sad is blue
And it tastes like water.
Sad smells like salt
And it looks like tears.
Sad sounds like someone playing the harp
And it feels like a cold block of ice.

Harriet Eason (11)
West Coker CE VC Primary School, Yeovil

Stress

Stress is a dark, dark green.
It tastes like bitter cheese
And smells like burning plastic.
Stress looks like a slimy water snake
And sounds like a high-pitched scream.
Stress feels like a rough brick.

Tom Sollars (10)
West Coker CE VC Primary School, Yeovil

Love

Love is the colour of a bright red apple
And tastes of chocolate ice cream.
It smells of freshly baked bread.
Love looks like a big heart
And sounds like the waves of the sea.
It feels silky soft.

Sarah Brady (9)
West Coker CE VC Primary School, Yeovil

Happiness

Happiness is yellow,
Happiness tastes like chips,
Happiness smells like pot pourri,
Happiness looks like the sun,
Happiness sounds like waves crashing against the rocks.
Happiness feels joyful.

Louise Goodland (10)
West Coker CE VC Primary School, Yeovil

Joy

Joy is orange
Joy tastes like strawberries
Joy smells like my mum
Joy looks happy
Joy sounds like children playing
Joy feels like fun.

Alexandra Barbaro (11)
West Coker CE VC Primary School, Yeovil

Hate

Hate is red
It tastes like hot curry
Hate smells like trouble
It is a jigsaw never completed
Hate sounds like bones breaking
It feels horrible!

Jack Cozens (10)
West Coker CE VC Primary School, Yeovil

Joy

Joy is the colour of a bunch of blueberries.
Joy tastes like bananas
And smells like a rose.
Joy looks like a sunset
And sounds like the chirping of a bird.
Joy feels like a silky peach.

Jared Wiseman (11)
West Coker CE VC Primary School, Yeovil

Love

Pink, pink, luminous pink is love
Love tastes like a chocolate dove
It smells like strawberry soap
It looks like a pink heart
It sounds like birds singing in the sky
Love feels like a furry heart.

Sam Harris (9)
West Coker CE VC Primary School, Yeovil

What Is The Sun?

The sun is a golden pancake
Tossed high in the sky.
It is a beautiful yellow balloon
Hovering behind the hills.

The sun is a glitter disco ball
Glittering in the clouds.
It is a golden sunflower
Stretched right into space.

The sun is a hot air balloon
Bobbing high in space.
It is an amber Smartie
Squashed between the clouds.

The sun is an orange Frisbee
Whizzing through the air.
It is a beautiful dandelion
Swaying through the clouds.

Chloe Partridge (8)
West Coker CE VC Primary School, Yeovil

Hate

Hate is the colour of a dark night
Hate is the taste of a bitter lollipop
Hate is the smell of my watch
Hate is the look of a dark room
Hate is the sound of a woman screaming
Hate makes me feel sad.

Jim Crisp (11)
West Coker CE VC Primary School, Yeovil

What Is The Sun?

The sun is a flying saucer
Spinning through the sky.
It is a big orange sunflower
Reaching up to Heaven.

The sun is a golden pancake
Spinning high in the sky.
It is a big yellow diamond
Shooting through the clouds.

The sun is a golden ruby
Filling the air.
It is a colourful football
Flying through the air.

The sun is a beautiful hot air balloon
Floating through the air.
It is a pink and purple planet
Jetting through space.

Bran Pick (7)
West Coker CE VC Primary School, Yeovil

Hate

Hate is black
Hate tastes like courgettes
Hate smells like dead rats
Hate looks like blood
Hate sounds like crying
Hate feels like cold metal.

Khan Green (7)
West Coker CE VC Primary School, Yeovil

What Is The Sun?

The sun is a diamond
Gleaming through the air.

The sun is a red-hot fireball
Zooming round in orbit.

The sun is a big red bubble
Bobbing up and down.

The sun is a big balloon
Floating in the galaxy.

The sun is a yellow Frisbee
Spinning round the planets.

The sun is like an explosion
Floating through space.

Elliot Boon (9)
West Coker CE VC Primary School, Yeovil

What Is The Sun?

The sun is a glittering fire diamond
Sparking through the sky.
It is a beautiful orange and yellow dandelion
Floating through space.

The sun is a flashing disco ball
Spinning through the clouds.
It is a colourful football
Burning all the Earth.

The sun is a yellow pancake
Skimming the air.
It is an orange Smartie
Flying in and out of space.

Amy Reddaway (9)
West Coker CE VC Primary School, Yeovil

What Is The Sun?

The sun is a yellow ball
Bouncing in the clouds.
It is a beautiful orange balloon
Floating through the air.

The sun is a burning fireball
Whizzing up in space.
It is a hot flying saucer
Spinning through the planets.

Robert Small (7)
West Coker CE VC Primary School, Yeovil

Happiness

Happiness is bright red.
Happiness tastes like strawberry.
Happiness smells like melted chocolate.
It looks like a garden full of roses.
It sounds like people laughing.
It feels like happiness.

Niki Thiella (8)
West Coker CE VC Primary School, Yeovil

Love - It Makes Sense!

Love is the colour red,
It tastes like strawberries and cream, ice cream,
It looks like a big, juicy heart,
It smells like roses and a box of chocolates,
It sounds like a romantic CD,
It feels like a big cuddly bear.

Daisy Copland (9)
West Coker CE VC Primary School, Yeovil

What Is The Sun?

The sun is a glittering diamond
Sparkling through the clouds.
It is an amber dandelion
Drifting through the breeze.

The sun is a golden sunflower
Bouncing above the hill.
It is a glittering disco ball
Tossed high in the sky.

The sun is an orange pancake
Drifting high and low.
It is an orange Smartie
Bobbing through space.

Molly Morris (7)
West Coker CE VC Primary School, Yeovil

Winter, Winter

Winter, winter, is so cold
Loads of men go really bold
Winter is full of ice
With the heating is very nice

We all get a lot of ice
Which we like, very nice
We love the snow
When it drops very low

The snow is very good
We can play like we should
We love the snow
It could be good if it could flow.

Sarah Campbell (9)
Weston Park Primary School, Lawrence Weston

Summer

Summer, summer, all around,
All the heatness would be found.
All we do is drink and drink,
When we're out of school
We don't have to think and think.

Good morning summer,
Goodnight winter.
All we do is think of water,
Summer wood could cause a splinter.

Summer is so hot,
We think of water a lot.
When we're in the paddling pool,
All we do is act like a fool.

Summer is really hot,
With all our friends we play.
I really like it on holiday,
When I go to a sandy bay.

Ewan Estcourt (9)
Weston Park Primary School, Lawrence Weston

Summertime

I like summer
It is so fun
I stay out for as long as I like
I would like a bun.

Summer, summer, I like summer
I am off all day
I enjoy the summer
I am gay in a happy way.

Ceri-Mai Shepherd (9)
Weston Park Primary School, Lawrence Weston

The Beach

The beach is fun
I like the sun.

The water's nice
It's like ice
The sand is hot
Just like a pot.

I just don't know what to do
I am writing this for you.

Summer is a happy time
People always read and rhyme
You'll be going out for a tan
But don't go eating too much ham.

I like having my birthday
In a kind of special way.

The sun is hot so I go out
I like going out and about
I like making sandcastles
Instead of making a hassle
I like playing with my toys
And I like making noise.

Summer is a happy time
People always read and rhyme
You'll be going out for a tan
Don't go eating too much ham.

Kara Houson (8)
Weston Park Primary School, Lawrence Weston

The Sun - Haiku

The sun is up high
Burning like a big fireball
In the blue, bright sky.

Jacob Hicks (8)
Weston Park Primary School, Lawrence Weston

Carrot Crunchers

Bunny rabbits hopping around
Stamping their feet on the ground
Having babies in their cage
Ripping paper of the page
In the wild they play with their friends
The fun never ends.

Alex McGill (9)
Weston Park Primary School, Lawrence Weston

Pets

They're very nice
With sugar and spice
You cuddle them
When you're there with them
Fluffy tails and fluffy heads
Lie down in your bed.

Lauren Ogden (8)
Weston Park Primary School, Lawrence Weston

Shiny

Shiny,
Shiny as a little star,
Shiny as the sun outside,
Shiny like the sun above you,
Shiny.

Kirsty Hannan (9)
Weston Park Primary School, Lawrence Weston

Sunshine

A lovely, shiny gold coin in the sky,
Waiting for the birds to fly by.

High, high up it goes,
Miles up there away from our toes.

We never wear jumpers, not ever,
Especially in this weather.

There's not much breeze,
But lots of leaves on the trees.

The gentle wind does not make falling leaves,
So the leaves won't fall on your knees.

Have a water fight with your friends,
Luckily the sun makes the day not end.

Mind the sun, it might get in your eyes,
In your room you might have flies.

Hannah Weekes (9)
Weston Park Primary School, Lawrence Weston

Baboon

A red but smelly breath
It's known to bring death
It eats nits
And it's got smelly armpits.

It lives in a cage
It's known to bring rage
It's got long fur
But it really doesn't purr.

Callum James (9)
Weston Park Primary School, Lawrence Weston

There Was An Old Lady

There was an old lady so feeble
Who wanted to do some evil.
She took Rapunzel so fair
And made her grow her hair.
The witch locked her in a tower
And Rapunzel waited hour by hour.
Every day the witch would say,
'Rapunzel, Rapunzel, let down your hair,
So I can climb the golden stair.'
The witch fed her on potato peelings
That really upset her feelings.
One day she sang a song
That made a young prince come along.
The prince heard her voice so sweet
And then decided they must meet.
He climbed his way through her hair
Then he said he could not bear
To live without her. No, he could not bear.
Then he heard the witch coming
Then you should have seen him running.
He jumped on his horse and sped away
'Rapunzel,' he bellowed, 'see you another day.'
The witch chopped off all her locks
So Rapunzel packed up all her frocks.
She went to find the prince
And said, 'Let's get married straight away.'
So they did and then rode off at the end of the day.

Esther Watson (9)
Wiveliscombe Primary School, Taunton

Jake's Pet Snake

There once was a boy called Jake,
Who had a big pet snake.
It bit his right hand,
Covered him in sand,
Then chucked him into the lake.

He swam away to the side,
Then took the local bus ride.
His snake tried to go,
Landed in snow,
Then got kicked by the guide.

He took a trip in a boat,
All the way to Limber Float,
Went for a swim,
Met his cross dad, Jim,
Then got hit by a goat.

The goat fell asleep,
He had a little weep,
Jim said, 'You are bad,'
He said, 'I thought you were a nice dad,'
And the snake was jumping like a sheep.

Then they caught the snake,
Hit it with a rake.
It got knocked out cold,
Though Jim was still bold,
Then they went home for a cake.

Charlie Mitchell (8)
Wiveliscombe Primary School, Taunton

My Brother Jonathan

My brother Jonathan,
Both sensible and smart,
Enjoying his Kingsmead,
(Especially art).

He's awkward and choosy
And careful with his pick,
He's a very noisy chatterbox,
Which sometimes makes me sick!

He's a daring young tantrum,
As a hurricane's gust,
He's very, very funny,
Although he makes a fuss.

He's a computer buff
And a fish wizkid too,
He's smarter than a scientist
(And honestly, it's true!)

Sophie Prescott (9)
Wiveliscombe Primary School, Taunton

Summer Has Come

The first morning of summer has come,
So we can dance and play in the sun.
We can swim through the beach's waves,
We can search dark and scary caves.

Dad's blowing up the paddling pool,
So we can have a dip and keep cool.
Splashing around getting everyone wet,
Please don't make us get out, not yet!

Rachael Bashford (10)
Wiveliscombe Primary School, Taunton

The Siege Of Troy

In Ancient Greece, in the siege of Troy,
The Greek soldiers hid in a horsey toy.
You're probably wondering how they did fit,
Well, this is the very interesting bit!
The horse was huge, humungous and hollow,
In its belly a few armoured soldiers did wallow.
With weapons a-ready those clever felons,
Tricked their way into Troy to rescue Helen.
Through the columned gates the horse was pulled,
The citizens of Troy were truly fooled!
They slashed their swords through the marathon task,
How many died? Please don't ask!
They captured Helen and took her away,
But alas there was no wedding day.
For Paris had been shot with poisoned dart
And they took him away in a hay bale cart.
So Helen returned to her loved one that day
And they didn't try again to take her away.

Jessica Robinson (10)
Wiveliscombe Primary School, Taunton

Snow

Snow
Snow is soft, silky and white
And looks like a blanket of daisies.
Snow is cold,
Like Antarctica frozen,
Snow, snow, snow.
Snow makes me feel the new year has come
And the sledges come out of the cupboards.
Snow represents winter,
Snow, snow, snow.

Laura Vercoe (11)
Wiveliscombe Primary School, Taunton

Let Me Help The Rhino

The rhino, silvery-grey walking on the sand,
His horn like a sharp razor knife,
He charges across an overgrown land,
But not knowing he will soon lose life,
Because when the heartless poachers come
To slaughter and to take,
Watching babies and rhino mum, drinking at the far lake,
We want it to stop, right here, right now,
But it just doesn't seem to work
And I see them, yes the rhinos bow
To us for help, we don't smirk,
They seem to be crying, 'We're endangered, help!'
But all I can think is, *how?*
I wish it could stop, they're heartless,
They come, they're poachers,
Stop right now!

Zoe Wilkes (10)
Wiveliscombe Primary School, Taunton

Star Wars

Twi'leks from Mars,
Droids from the stars,
Spacecraft from Pluto,
Astromechs from Kabuto.

Jedi from the farthest moon,
Like Qui Gon Jinn and Plo Koon,
The Jedi academy on Yavin 4,
Apprentices training more and more.

Jedi knights and Jedi masters,
Clones and X-wings equipped with blasters,
The Millennium Falcon with secret spice stores,
This and much more, all part of *Star Wars!*

Andrew Fudge (9)
Wiveliscombe Primary School, Taunton

My Brother Fraser

I have a brother
His real name is Frizz
But we all love him dearly
Although he's a tractor wiz.

I think he's sweet
So do Mum and Dad
But sometimes we don't like him
Because he is really bad.

He loves his climbing
Up the climbing wall
Daddy helps him up
Because he's very small.

Now this is not all true
Because my brother is sweet
Although he kicks me
With very freezing feet.

Rosie Johnson (9)
Wiveliscombe Primary School, Taunton

The Big Dragon

I once saw a big dragon out of the zoo,
It ran around madly looking for you!
It looked at some people and said, 'No, no, no!
The person I'm looking for might be called Joe.'
He couldn't find him so he yelled, 'That is that!'
And he jumped up high and squashed someone flat!
Then a young boy called Nathan Mac Ho,
Explained that the boy he squashed was called Joe.
The dragon was angry, as angry as could be
And then he died because he hit a tree!

Ben Salter (8)
Wiveliscombe Primary School, Taunton

The Special Places

There are special places we all go to rest,
Where our dreams are formed, some of the best,
Where witches can fly and dragons can roar,
Where giant birds live and phoenixes soar.

Use your imagination and be what you want,
Where *capital* letters are *capital* font,
And shapes say hello and the sun says goodbye,
Where animals can talk and giants lie.

The jungle, the sea, are places you can go,
Or go to the airport where planes can fly low,
And pyramids are shaped like an ice cream cone,
Where you can go - don't need to phone.

You can dream what you want in your own special land,
You could go to the beach and feel the sand,
'Cause we all have our own special place to go,
We can be what we like, what we like we can do.

Vicky Bendall (10)
Wiveliscombe Primary School, Taunton

Lions

Lions are mighty, fierce and brave,
Like some bears in a cave,
And getting ready to stalk their prey,
Watching a deer sit down to lay,
And creeping like a mouse with cheese,
Catching a scent from the rushing breeze,
They chase and pounce like bullets from a gun,
Then they rest in the beautiful sun,
After eating a delicious meal,
They will never know how scared others feel,
When they are around the lions.

Fiona Hamilton (10)
Wiveliscombe Primary School, Taunton

Pilot Fred

There once was a pilot called Fred,
Who thought that his plane was his bed.
He slept through a war
And fell on the floor,
When he got up he banged his head.

So Fred then climbed into his plane
And went soaring up through the rain,
He fired his gun
And shot down his son
And he was in terrible pain.

His son he managed to pull through
And so within a year or two,
He wanted revenge,
So he went to Stonehenge,
A plan came to him that was new.

He gathered twenty or so fleas,
But he knew they had no disease.
To his father's shock,
He soon saw the flock
And thought they were miniature bees!

Jack Cowling (10)
Wiveliscombe Primary School, Taunton

Cadbury's Creme Eggs - Haiku

Cadbury's Creme Eggs,
Taste deliciously like eggs,
Cadbury's Creme Eggs.

Steven Grabham (10)
Wiveliscombe Primary School, Taunton

Matt Hat

There was a young man called Matt Hat,
Who played with a ball and a bat,
He swung hard at the ball,
Which hit a low wall
And flattened the neighbour's fat cat.

His neighbour looked over the wall
And was hit in the face by the ball,
He let out a loud roar,
That reached the seashore
And Matt Hat felt half an inch tall.

Matt said to the neighbour, 'Sorry,'
But then he started to worry,
The neighbour threw the ball,
Which again hit the wall
And Matt escaped in his lorry.

Jack Humphries (10)
Wiveliscombe Primary School, Taunton

The Fantasy Castle

The fantasy castle with big, creeping walls,
Up in the sky the dragons will call,
Prancing pixies and witches on brooms,
In the tower where ghosts howl and loom!

Vikings and soldiers, fighting on grass,
A beautiful maid riding on a brown ass,
A three-headed snake spitting its venom,
After that went to pick a gold lemon.

Princes and princesses, queens and the king,
The golden bell that goes *dong, dong, ding, ding!*
All in a place where the houses are big
And all the people have turned into pigs.

Hannah Stone (11)
Wiveliscombe Primary School, Taunton

From A Tank Turret

Faster than cheetahs, faster than thunder,
Corpses and camps, pass without blunder,
Charging along like a furious rhino,
Crushing trenches like plastic lino:
All the sights of death and pain,
Thundering through the lashing rain
And ever again in the roar of the battle,
Enemies lie like slaughtered cattle:
Here is a corporal who lies in pain,
Like a dragon, finally slain,
Here is a sergeant who screams out orders
And there is a trench by the enemy borders.
Here is a gun destroyed in the rain
And there is a corpse with a blood-red stain.
What did the world do to deserve such a fate?
For the scene of war is easy to hate.

Andrew Heard (10)
Wiveliscombe Primary School, Taunton

The Shores Of The Pond

The fish turns, leaps, dives down to the sandy bottom
By the driftwood that is old and rotten
Weaves and swims through pond weed thick
Like a cheetah, deadly quick.
The frog hops and drops down into the weed
As the heron watches through the reeds.
The dragonflies hover, then perch upon the tops
Of the lily pads, then sit on the cold, hard rocks.
The miniature lizard scuttles through the small stones
As the whirlwind of winds starts to moan and then groans.

Rhianna White (10)
Wiveliscombe Primary School, Taunton